The Secret Karate Techniques
Kata Bunkai

Warning

The techniques described in this book and the techniques of any martial art are dangerous. You should, therefore, train under the supervision of an expert. Please also use caution when handling or using any weapons and consult a qualified teacher. Please use restraint when practicing techniques described in this book. Neither the author nor the publishers of this book are responsible for the results of your choice to practice these techniques. Please respect the law and order of your country.

Helmut Kogel

THE SECRET
KARATE TECHNIQUES
KATA BUNKAI

Meyer & Meyer Sport

Original title: Kata Bunkai – Die geheimen Techniken im Karate
© 2010 Meyer & Meyer Verlag

Translated by Judy Keenan

The Secret Karate Techniques
Kata Bunkai
Helmut Kogel
Maidenhead: Meyer & Meyer Sport (UK) Ltd., 2010
ISBN: 978-1-84126-289-5

© 2010 by Meyer & Meyer Verlag, Aachen
Aachen, Adelaide, Auckland, Budapest, Cape Town, Graz, Indianapolis,
Maidenhead, Olten (CH), Singapore, Toronto
Member of the World
Sport Publishers' Association (WSPA)
www.w-s-p-a.org
Printed by: B.O.S.S Druck und Medien GmbH
ISBN: 978-1-84126-289-5
E-Mail: info@m-m-sports.com
www.m-m-sports.com

Contents

Introduction

This book has been written for all those interested in the Martial Arts and who want to look more deeply into the material behind authentic Okinawan Karate. Knowledge of the background behind Okinawa's Martial Arts is not widespread, particularly with regard to the stimulation of vital points (Jintai Kyusho). Demonstrations for the use of single Kata sequences (Bunkai) often stagnate at the surface of the Martial Arts (Omote), yet it is important for advanced students to realize and have access to the finer points of Karate which are worth the effort and the years of intensive training needed to know them.

Whereas, in the past, secret Okinawan Karate techniques were passed on solely to a chosen few, modern media now make it possible to make contact with numerous research groups active in investigating the background and essence of Karate and, above all, its application.

During a journey to Okinawa several years ago, I became acquainted with Master Tetsuhiro Hokama (10th Dan Goju Ryu Karate, Hanshi). He challenged me to undertake a project to further investigate the medical-physiological underpinnings of Karate (vital point stimulation). He explained that, although it is common knowledge that Jintai Kyusho is effective, no one knows exactly how it functions. He was hopeful that I would be able to shed more light on the working mechanisms of Kyusho, knowing that I was a medical doctor as well as a Master of Karate.

It became obvious to me that if I was to succeed, I would have to look very closely at material about Chinese Acupuncture. This study took several years and uncovered facts which led to a significant advance in understanding Okinawan Karate. My research work was compiled into a large, but not published, compendium which was made available to Dr. T. Hokama.

To prevent the hidden knowledge held in the traditional Karate Kata from being lost, we decided to decode numerous movement sequences as far as this was possible. To this end, Master Hokama assumed responsibility for Goju Ryu Karate and I assumed responsibility for the background of the Shuri Te and Shotokan Kata. In our work together we were able to compile many details and could incorporate the preparatory work done by other international working groups (see Literature).

Among the most important pioneers in this area are: Patrick Mc Carthy, George Dillman, Evan Pantazi and his employees, as well as Erle Montaigue, Ian Abernethy and Werner Lind's research group. The changes and modifications made over the centuries to the original movements obviously made interpretation more difficult. In this book I have tried to illustrate the relationship between the Tuite- **(levers)** and the Jintai Kyusho **(sensitive points)** techniques and modern human anatomy.

Even so, it was not possible to cover the entire spectrum of ancient knowledge as this would have overstepped the framework of a normal book and also the capabilities of one single person. We had to restrict ourselves to a few examples of Kata sequences. For those interested in expanding their knowledge and enhancing their abilities with the applications described and illustrated in this book, I recommend taking part in seminars held by various working groups. I wish the reader success and enjoyment with the book and feel certain that there are many who will now see the Martial Arts from a different point of view. Perhaps ... this book will be a catalyst for motivating further research on the background of the Kata applications.

Acknowledgements

"Such is the way that a Master lives out his life, aware of his imperfection, never satisfied with his abilities even to his final day, neither vain nor condescending" (Quotation from Hagakure, by Tsunetomo Yamamoto).

I would not like to neglect thanking my teachers, who have accompanied me on my way in the Martial Arts, for their efforts, their patience and the most precious time spent together. They are: Hans-Dieter Rauscher, 8th Dan Shotokan Karate Hanshi, 7th Dan Iaido Kyoshi, 6th Dan Kobudo Kyoshi, 8th Antas Arnis , Ikio Higushi, 9th Dan Gimma-Ha Ryu Karate Hanshi, 7th Dan Kobudo Kyoshi, Kazuo Sakai, 10th Dan Wado Ryu Hanshi, 8th Dan Kempo Hanshi, 8th Dan Kobudo Hanshi, Professor Shizuya Sato, 10th Dan Nihon Jujutsu Hanshi, 9th Dan Judo Hanshi, Hirokatsu Kanazawa 10th Dan Shotokan Karate Hanshi and many others.

My gratitude goes out, in particular, to Tetsuhiro Hokama Dr. Dr., 10th Dan Goju Ryu Karate, Kobudo, Kyusho Hanshi, who encouraged me to examine the physiological **background** and consequences of Karate and its Kata. It was through him that I became acquainted with the Martial Arts as they are lived on Okinawa, the cradle of Karate. It was he who helped me to achieve deeper insight into the history of Okinawan Te.

My thanks, also, to my sons Marc (3rd Dan Karate, 1st Dan Bo Jutsu) and Lutz (3rd Dan Karate) for their help in putting this book together. To my son, Marc, and my Karate students: "Thank you for your assistance with corrective work on the manuscript." A very large "thank you" to my wife, Elvira, for all her help in assembling the photos and to the employees of the Meyer & Meyer publishing company who have, as usual, produced an excellent layout and end product. Thanks also to Judy Keenan for the translation from German to English.

Preface

What is the Essence of Karate?

By Tetsuhiro Hokama

Karate is a defensive Martial Art which in earlier times developed on the Ryukyu Island as Te (English "Hand"). Basically, Te is an instinctive self-defense against enemy forces which threaten one's own existence. The original form of Te is also known as Temai (English: dancing hand). Temai is essentially a form of reflex-based self-defense when under attack. This form developed further into what is known as Karate today.

The Spirit of Karate and the Way

Karate means daily training of one's mind and body and paying attention to one's own health. Ideally, self-defense against an attacker is carried out, unarmed, in an emergency situation, although in certain situations a Karate fighter is permitted to make use of a weapon. There is one important rule in Karate: "Neither should one be hit, nor should one cause harm to another."

The fundamental idea is to resolve a conflict in a peaceful manner. Put another way: An enemy attack should not be worth its while in Karate. The philosophy of Karate was developed further as a means of teaching self control. In the latter part of the 1920's Karate was renamed to "Karate-Do" (Art of the Empty Hand).

The History of Karate

It has been suggested that the art of fist fighting originated in the regions of Mesopotamia and parts of North Turkey and reached the Ryukyu Island by way of the Silk Road to India and China. There is also another theory which suggests this style of combat travelled over the seas to reach Japan by way of Indonesia and South East Asia.

Legend has it that the Indian monk, **Bodhidharma (jp. Daruma)**, founder and the first patriarch of Zen Buddhism, arrived at the Shaolin monastery on the Songshan mountain in Henan Province around the year 526 and was also a practitioner of the Martial Arts. These basic elements of Shaolin Martial Arts continued to be developed and further spread by the monastery. Daruma is honored in Japan as the Patron of the Ryukyu School of Karate.

He wrote two Sutras, Yi-jin-jing (Transformation of the Tendons and Ligaments, Various Breathing Techniques for Improving Stamina) and Xi-sui-jing (Ablution of the Marrow to Develop Self-Discipline and Inner Strength). Bohdidharma is also supposed to have drawn up the Wu-De (Principles of the Virtues of the Martial Arts) which teaches discipline, self-control, modesty and a respect for life. Once it became obvious that those who trained according to these principles were more successful in self-defense, this then led to further development. The ancient style was gradually complemented by elements of dance and, of course, additional techniques for self-defense. There are several legends regarding the transit route of the Shaolin Martial Arts to the Ryukyu Island. One thing is certain: the teachings of Bodhiharma were to have the decisive influence on Ryukyu-Karate-Do.

The Spread of Karate to Japan's Main Island

The first major Japanese Budo Association (Dai Nippon Butokukai) was founded in Kyoto in 1895. In the interest of establishing uniform qualifications, it was decided to set up examinations and qualification tests for three levels: the Master Certificate (Hanshi), Teacher (Kyoshi) and Apprentice (Renshi). Judo and Kendo were introduced into the curriculum of higher schools. This was a requirement to enable these traditional Martial Arts to reach a larger audience.

In its home country of Okinawa, however, Karate remained a closed book for the general public as the Martial Arts were passed down solely within the inner family circle. It was Kanryo Higaonna, a Master from Naha, who opened the first Karate Dojo in Naha in 1889 after his return from China. Anko Itosu (a Master from Shuri) began to train primary school pupils in Shuri in 1901. Karate's existence as an Okinawan Martial Art became known on the main island of Honshu through demonstrations in schools. This was later followed by an invitation to take part in a sport demonstration organized by the **Ministry of Education**. Two Masters, Funakoshi and Isoma, demonstrated Okinawa's Karate during a major show in Tokyo in 1922. The first book on Karate was released by Master Funakoshi in November of the same year. In 1924 Karate Master Funakoshi started up a working group at the Keio University with the aid of the famous Judo founder, Master Jigoro Kano, and other renowned Judo and Kendo Masters. Additional Karate study groups were also established at Tokyo University and the Takushoku University. The Main Karate Student Society (founded in 1936) helped to spread the art of Okinawan Karate to Japan's main island. The newspapers of the day printed sensational reports about Choki Motobu, a Karate Master from Shuri, who had knocked out a foreign professional boxer in the ring. In 1927 Chojun Miyagi, Master and Founder of Goju Ryu, began giving Karate courses at universities such as the

Ritsumei and the Kyoto University. Kanbun Uechi, a Master of Uechi Ryu who had just returned from China, founded a Dojo in Wakayama shi, in western Japan. Compared to Judo and Kendo, Karate was not as well-known in Japan at this stage. However its spread was aided by the elite circles reached through courses at the universities. Karate's Kanji style of writing was changed around 1905. **This was a prerequisite of the acceptance in Japan.** Karate was finally recognized by the Japanese Traditional Sport Society as an official Traditional Sport/Art in 1933.

Up until 1925 the art of Karate on Okinawa was not as structured as the comparable Martial Arts of Judo or Kendo. It had neither a direction of style nor so-called "schools". It was restricted to three different forms of Te: Shuri-Te, Naha-Te and Tomari-Te. Naha-Te was renamed Goju Ryu (School) in 1929. Shuri-Te became Kobayashi Ryu in 1933 and in 1939 the Shotokan School absorbed Shuri-Te. Handansui Ryu was changed to Kamichi Ryu in 1940. Over time other Karate Schools (Ryu-Ha) such as Shito Ryu, Sento Ryu, Wado Ryu and Kyokushin Kai Karate emerged. The origin and development of Okinawan Karate is not identical with other traditional Japanese fighting techniques, the philosophies of which are bedded in the spiritual substance of the Samurai. Okinawa's Karate Art has not only had a major influence on traditional Japanese Martial Arts, but has also spread rapidly in the USA and around the rest of the world since 1950. Karate, which came from the small island of Okinawa, has become a movement of worldwide proportions.

Karate is not only physical but also mental training. Its exercises lead to a harmonious balance in life.

Tetsuhiro Hokama, Dr. Ph.D
10th Dan Goju-Ryu Karate, Hanshi
President of Goju-Ryu Kenshikai
Curator of the Okinawan Karate Museum, Uehara Nishihara

A. General Part:
An Overview

1 The Historical Development of Okinawan Karate

Okinawa's Social Structure and the Origin of its Martial Arts

For the original inhabitants of Okinawa Island the word Oki meant "sea". Like a "cloak" (nawa), this island seemed to have been cast over the surface of the sea (Okinawa). The Chinese referred to it as Ryu Kyu (Lyu Kyu). The island itself was under the rule of the many lords of the Anji Dynasty until the end of the 11th century A.D. While a myriad of myths surround the first King, Tenson, the first "official" King was Shunten (1187). During the fourth generation of the Tamagusuku Period, three independent kingdoms emerged: Hokuzan in the north, Nanzan in the south, and the central region of Chuzan. Central rule remained in the hands of Tamagusuku. This era is known as Okinawa's Period of Warring States. In 1337, during the Ming Dynasty, King Satto of Chuzan (from the citadel of Urasoe) sent a delegation to China as well as to neighboring countries to study their forms of martial arts with the aim of strengthening his own military forces. The kings of the northern and southern regions, however, had the same idea and did likewise. Chusan sent a delegation of 52 men to study the art of military battle, Nanzan sent eighteen and Hokuzan a group of nine. Military knowledge of other Asian countries, the art of battle with and without weapons, was integrated into the

Okinawa´s Shuri Castle (Exhibition Model)

kingdom in this way and put into practical use. It has been surmised that this was perhaps the origin of the ensuing art of Karate. Several years later King Hashi of Chuzan was able to defeat the opposing kingdoms and unite the country. This increased and reinforced his military power and he then moved his seat of government to Shuri, in the vicinity of the important ports of Naha and Tomari.

Reinforcement of Shuri Castle on Okinawa

China harshly criticized Okinawa during the wars. Having united his country under one rule, King Hashi was able to negotiate agreements with China which enabled not only cultural exchange but also the exchange of commercial and military wares. This became a period of intensive commercial trade with China, Japan, South East Asia and Korea. During the rule of various lords of the Sho Dynasty, military experts occupied themselves with nothing other than martial arts. As a means of preventing rebellion among the aristocracy, a total of 38 families (Udun) with royal blood were relocated to the area surrounding the royal palace in Shuri. The Udun, the highest caste, were given roughly 3300 square meters in the western section of Shuri. A lower caste, the Uekata (Oyakata), was also awarded land by the King as a reward for their services.

Both castes were in possession of their own land and were in charge of the caste below them, the Chikudun Pechin. These, in turn, were in charge of the caste of the Satunushi Peichin. The lower class Chikudun Peichin was basically responsible for ensuring security and upholding the law. Soldiers (Bushi) in the Ryu Kyu Kingdom could be divided into five different groups. The first group, the Shuri Warriors (Shuri Bushi), was responsible for the defense of Shuri Castle. A second group, the Tomari (Tomari Bushi), was primarily there to enforce law and order. The third group (Naha Bushi) was entrusted with the protection of Chinese delegates (Sappushi) and the trading ships which were sent from Ryu Kyu to China. Yet another group, Udun Bushi, was involved in the political activities of the Regency. The fifth and remaining group was comprised of soldiers (Bushi) of the Chinese enclave near Naha, known as Kumemura. They were trusted with providing protection for and aiding Chinese immigrants.

The 36 Chinese Families in Kume

Between 1392 and 1393 Chinese settlers, primarily officials and tradesmen, were moved to Okinawa at the request of the Chinese Government. Though history books refer to: "The 36 families," the number "36" is a symbolic number used as a Chinese figure of speech and should not be taken literally. Reference was also made to the "36 Families of Fukien" and the "hundred names from China." The aim of Chinese settlement was to import Chinese cultural characteristics into Okinawa and thereby

Reproduction of the first Chinese Settlement of the 36 Families in Kume

help the island's inhabitants to optimally organize their daily lives according to what was then seen as the modern ideal. Obviously this was not entirely without self-interest. China had high hopes of a flourishing trade in commercial goods and also of establishing a certain political influence on the island. China also demanded payment of a toll twice a year in the form of commercial goods. The first Chinese Delegate (Sappushi) travelled to the islands of Ryu Kyu in 1404. The inhabitants of the Ryu Kyu islands are to this day grateful for having learned from

Monument for the 36 Families of Kumemura

China and do not regret the investment made in the past. For a very long time they readily paid their tribute to both China and to Japan. Even today China's strong influence can be seen in Okinawa's architecture and in its culture. The traditional Dragon Boat Race (Hatju-Sen), which still takes place every year on Okinawa, originated in the year 1400, and is very popular in the south of China. The Kumemura settlement on Okinawa is still definitely a tourist attraction worth seeing.

An important factor for the development of what came to be Karate was that the Chinese Delegates (Sappushi) were accompanied to Okinawa by their bodyguards, who then passed on the Chinese Art of Self Defense to the inhabitants of the island. Among the 36 families there were several people of importance for Okinawa, such as Cai, Zeng, Mao, Liang, Jin, Chen, Wu, Rin and Yuan. (For more

Furu Helin, the cave between Naha and Tomari

detail see Chapter 5). All of these names are strongly connected to the martial arts. Over the centuries there was assimilation of the Chinese families into Okinawa's culture and a Chinese influence on Okinawa as well.

According to Hokama, it was the Zheng Yiyi family who brought Chinese Boxing and the secret writings of the "Bubishi" to the Ryu Kyu islands. This particular style of Chinese Boxing may possibly have been the pioneer of the Naha Te. In 1608 the Zheng family began to teach the art of combat techniques in Kume. Hokama (Yabu) Peichin was known on Okinawa as a combative arts expert in 1644. There were also strong ties with other countries such as Korea, India, the Philippines and Taiwan. The many typhoons which hit Okinawa each year brought with them a large number of shipwrecks and many survivors who made it to the island's coast. Between Tomari and Naha was an "old cave", Furu Helin, in which Korean shipwreck survivors sought shelter in 1456. Such survivors are also believed to have instructed Okinawa's inhabitants in martial arts. It is believed that a total of over 1400 Chinese ships were wrecked off the coast of Okinawa. The cave mentioned above provided shelter time and time again for many shipwreck survivors, among them possibly Channan, Chinto and other known martial arts experts.

Udundi, the Secret Royal Martial Art

Udun means "royal or palace" and Di means "hand". Udundi means the Palace Hand or the Hand of the Royal House. Its origins go back to the Motobu family which can be traced back to the second Sho Dynasty (5th Son of King Sho Shitsu, Prince Sho Koshin Motobu Oji Chohei 1648-1668). This is the equivalent of the Second Period during which a ban was introduced on the use of weapons. From this time on, in the aristocratic Motobu family, particular Martial Arts were passed on only to the eldest son. Training began at the age of six years and consisted of training without weapons, with punching and kicking. The second phase incorporated training in the use of weapons. The systematization and naming of the Martial Art Udundi is attributed to Motobu Chohei (see above).

It can be compared with Taiji-Jutsu. The **first** phase consists of training hard techniques without weapons, similar to the hard Qigong. Its aim is to put the opponent or enemy out of commission using only an effective technique. Higher skills are taught later. They entail softer techniques such as the Tuite (Chinese: Tuishou), similar to the elements in soft Qigong. The key factor is the transfer of the essence of the art of sword fighting into the weaponless Combat Art of the Udundi. The soft dancing movements may initially appear ineffective to the lay-person even though they contain a combination of both hard and fast techniques.

This style of fighting is often not recognized as being as dangerous as it is despite its complete system of punches, kicks, close combat and use of weapons. Defense using everyday utensils is also incorporated with the aim of controlling the opponent without causing serious harm.

In Tuidi Jutsu we differentiate between Tuidi Gaeshi (deflecting) and Ura Gaeshi (reversed techniques). The highest level is Ajikata nu Mekata, which means "The Dance of the Feudal Lords." The perfect rendition of this Martial Art (called Mai) is typified by the absence of the usual combative position and the presence of a naturally upright stance with straightened knees. A further aim is to avoid close combat as much as possible, as this wastes energy and entails increased danger when faced with several opponents. Rapid evasive movements in the opponents' blind spot should enable defensive tactics against several opponents.

The Art of Udundi also has other important guiding principles such as not allowing aggression to occur, taking care of one's appearance and maintaining correct social behavior, and is built on the basis of well-ordered family relationships and a multifaceted occupation. Harmony within the family is an absolute prerequisite for practice of the Martial Arts. Regular practice of the Martial Arts should in no way have a negative effect on either family or job.

Udundi was passed on secretly and solely to the eldest son in a family. It was only in the 19th Century that the son of Motobu Choyu rejected this inheritance and refused to learn the traditional Martial Art of Udundi. It was the first break in this family tradition. Motobu Choju chose to teach a student who did not belong to the aristocracy to prevent this Art from disappearing. This student was Uehara Seikichi (1903- 2003), whom he chose in preference to his brother Choki Motobu as the latter was known for his violent and unpredictable temperament.

Uehara Seikichi honored the Motobu family by changing the name of this Martial Art **style** to Motobu-Ryu. He founded the All Okinawan Karate Kobudo Rengokai. Later, the eldest son of Choki Motobu, Motobu Chômei, asked Uehara Seikichi to teach him, so that he could return the Martial Art to the Motobu family. Even though Udundi was practiced in secret, it still found its way over various routes into Okinawa's Martial Arts.

Toudi, the Chinese Hand

Toudi is known on Okinawa as the Chinese Hand. It refers to a large number of styles of Chinese Martial Arts which became integrated into Okinawa's already existing Martial Arts system. Okinawa's typical martial arts were significantly influenced by the weapons ban under Satsuma rule. This was the case for these styles: The Cai Family Boxing, The Wu Xiangui (Go Kenki 1886-1940), The Crane Style and The Tang Daiji (To Daiki 1887-1944), the style of the Zheng Family. Hokama writes that the Kata Wanshu and Rohai were probably introduced by the Tang Daiji family.

Okinawa's Martial Art Style was also significantly influenced by the bodyguards assigned to the Delegates as can be seen in the Wanshu and Kushanku Kata. But the integration of Chinese Martial Arts into Okinawa's style was only a beginning. Okinawa's Martial Arts have continued to develop further over the centuries to become an extremely effective independent system.

Shuri Te, Tomari Te, Naha Te

Shuri Te

Okinawa's various settlements had already developed their own differing combative styles at an early stage. Shuri di or Shuri Te was a style which was practiced in areas close to Shuri Castle and refers to the style used by the guards of the castle complex. These guards were responsible for transporting the Chinese Emperor's toll to China twice a year, which meant that they often traveled on horseback from the castle complex. This was the origin of the Rider's Stance (Kiba Dachi) and the fast, powerful movements. Shuri Te was also strongly influenced by the Shaolin Kempo of north China. The style itself can be attributed to Itosu Anko, Teacher of Gichin Funakoshi.

Tomari Te

Tomari is located in the area lying between Naha and Shuri. In this area it was necessary for the guards to protect boats travelling between Naha's harbor and Shuri Castle. Their style was, of necessity, influenced by the narrow boats they used – and if it came to the worst, on which they had to fight. This style was particularly influenced by Matsumora Kosaku, and, later, by his student Motobu-Choki. It was typified by its tight stances and special techniques for fighting in close quarters. The actual Martial Art style of Tomari Te, however, has been lost for the most part.

Naha Te

Naha-Di or Naha Te, as it is known, was practiced by those responsible for protecting the commercial harbors against pirates. Naha Te was heavily influenced by the fighting methods of the Quanfa from the Chinese Province of Fujian. It was often compared to the Chinese Hand (Toudi). The typical stance in Sanchin Dachi and Naifuanchi Dachi was allegedly born of the necessity to maintain firm footing on a boat. The Naha Te techniques used for combat in close quarters were also typical and necessary for fighting against pirates on the narrow boats. Higashionna Kanryo was later an important Master of this style. His student, Miyagi Chojun, later changed the name Naha Te to Goju Ryu (hard-soft style). The basic elements still remain in Goju Ryu.

Okinawa Te arrives on Japan's Main Island - Styles (Ryuha)

Styles themselves were first defined and named after 1929. A differentiation was only seen as being necessary with the introduction of Okinawa's Martial Arts to the main island of Japan. It would have been exceedingly difficult to spread Karate on the main island without naming the style. Japan's traditional Martial Arts were strictly ordered into distinctive stylistic directions and this, too, was expected of other systems of combat. It was during this period that Okinawa Te came to be known as Karate (Empty Hand) this also being an homage to Japan although the ideograms clearly show the relationship to the Chinese Hand. With the aim of providing an ideological background to the Martial Arts, elements were adopted from Zen Buddhism and the name Karate Do (Way of the Empty Hand) was created. Numerous performances and publications helped Okinawa's ancient Martial Arts to become popular under the name of Karate. The spread of Karate on Japan's main island is intimately connected with the names Gichin Funakoshi (Shotokan Ryu), Gimma Makoto (Shuri Te, Gimma Ryu), Egami Shigeru, Choki Motobu (Motobu Ryu), Mabuni Kenwa (Shito Ryu), Gogen Yamagushi (Goju Ryu), Ohtsuka Hironori (Wado Ryu), Konishi Yasuhiro (Shindo Jinen Ryu) and many others. There are more than 150 recognized styles of Karate to date.

The Expansion of Karate Worldwide

Karate first came to be known throughout the world, however, after it had developed and changed in the direction of a sport. It was necessary to introduce Karate as a competitive sport and to establish an appropriate system of rules for it to achieve worldwide popularity. The number of students spread rapidly. In sharp contrast to times past when it was purely a system of combat, a matter of life and death, it had shifted its focus to the winning of points (Kumite Shiai) and the contest of Form (Kata Shiai). Emphasis was placed on aesthetic form, a flawless technique, athletic execution and an appreciation of the content of the Kata. Distinctions are made between three different types of contests: contest with no contact, semi-contact and full contact. As with boxing, it was necessary to develop not only a system of rules but also protective clothing (Mabuni Kenwa) to avoid serious injury. Many Japanese Masters have been of very great service in the development of Karate as a sport. Among them are: Masatoshi Nakayama, Hidetaka Nishiyama, Mas Oyama and many others. Full Contact Karate is practiced in Kyukushin Karate (M. Oyama), Koshiki (Hard Style) Karate and several other groups. Non Contact Karate has been perfected by the JKA (Japanese Karate Association) and the JKF (Japanese Karate Federation). Freestyle contests with protective clothing are typical for the Nihon Kenpo style, for example. Currently, there is an interest in Karate's secret techniques and all they offer.

2   Understanding the Kata

The appreciation of Karate and its Kata has grown enormously over the last 100 to 200 years. Although Karate was almost unknown outside Okinawa at the start of the 20th century, it has spread by way of Japan over the last 100 years to become known over the whole world. In the days when Karate, or Okinawa Ti, was confined to the archipelago of the Ryu Kyu Islands, Kata usually contained a Karate Master's entire combative system. These were expanded upon over generations with the specialized interpretations of new Master students. Instruction in the Kata was an important part of the combative system and was taken very seriously.

The Naihanchi (in Shotokan Tekki-) Kata 1-3, for example, were derived from one Kata which contained approximately 300 different movements. This division into Kata 1-3 was made for practical educational reasons as it made it easier for students to learn and enabled them to better perfect and apply them.

The original Naihanchi Kata was an elementary kata in Choki Motobu's (1870-1944) combat system and was taught in all of Okinawa's styles. Later, this kata was practiced in most styles, with the exception of Goju Ryu. The Naihanchi Kata contain various techniques, particularly those needed for close combat. As these three Kata have a relatively demanding and high technical level, the Shorin-Ryu (and later Shotokan Karate) practice the Heian Kata as alternatives which are somewhat easier in their execution. The level of technical difficulty in the Heian Kata (formerly Pinan) was increased to the level of Heian Godan. Itosu Anko considered this modification to be necessary after introducing Karate into the primary school curriculum. This moved the focus of practicing the Kata in the direction of physical education and sports. The self-defense aspect faded into the background. The majority of the higher Kata were not suitable for teaching in schools.

Until now the Masters had differentiated between the obvious, or public use (Omote), personal interpretations (Oyo Bunkai) and the secret techniques (Okuden). The secret techniques remained unknown to the majority of students; only advanced Masters were introduced to the secret techniques of the Kata by their teachers. They were only ever passed on in direct contact, no written documents were made. The Okuden techniques are not even mentioned in the books of Okinawan Masters such as Choki Motobu, Gichin Funakoshi (1886 or 1870-1957), Chojun Miyagi (1888-1953) and others.

Due to the fact that certain drills from the various Kata could only be learned with knowledge of secret techniques, Masters deliberately sought out students whom

Center left Choki Motobu, center right Seikichi Odo (Museum T. Hokama)

they believed to be particularly trustworthy. On the other hand, this meant that when no suitable student was available, a Master might well have kept his techniques to himself and taken his secrets with him to his grave. The tradition of only passing secret techniques on to particularly special students is still current practice. It was made possible for a great deal of knowledge to eventually reach the western world as one or two Okinawan Masters passed their secrets on to very special students from other cultures. One example of this is George Dillman's working group, whose knowledge was passed on by Soken Hohan (1891-1982). Patrick McCarthy, too, is attributed with important pioneer work in this area. Martial arts experts from Kyushu International, with various backgrounds in Karate Jutsu, Aikido, have made great progress in recent years with their research on secret techniques. They are: Evan Pantazi, Jim Corn, Mark Cline, and Gary Rooks. Pioneer work has been and is still being done. Earle Montaigue is intensively involved in studies of Dim Mac in Kata of the Chinese Martial Arts.

The inclusion of medical knowledge of the body, its joints and Chinese acupuncture enables such groups to decipher Karate techniques at a high level. This also applies to working groups such as that of Patrick McCarthy's working group, whose interest

Evan Pantazi (Kyusho International, center) during a course in Darmstadt, Germany, in 2008

was centered on the old system of Karate (Uchinada Karate) and researching the "Bubishi." They were able to shed more light on the Bunkai of the Kata. Even a performance of the Kata by the old Okinawan Masters gave no such profound knowledge over the uses of the techniques from an acupuncture point of view. The true background of the single Kata sequences remained invisible to the layperson and the beginner. It was knowledge of the so-called secret techniques which turned harmless self-defense into a decisive end-technique in a potentially fatal situation. This was most probably the original idea of the Kata of Okinawa's Masters.

The introduction of Karate into schools on Japan's main island made it necessary for Karate to become acceptable as a sport. This, in turn, meant that the entire system needed to be refurbished and developed. It was logical to follow the lead from the work done by Jigoro Kano in Judo. The first adjustments were made by Gichin Funakoshi. Dangerous techniques were eliminated and other techniques modified, sometimes to the extent that they were no longer easily recognizable. Many open-hand techniques were turned into closed-hand (fist) movements, analogous to popular boxing. The Kata were modified with, respectively the low stance of Shotokan Karate, drawing back the rear hand, the drawn back hip (Hikite) and the occasional modification of the Mai Geri into a Yoko Geri. This resulted in a more sportsman-like and athletic presentation of the techniques, which was very important for demonstrating Karate at world competitions. It also allowed for a scale of criteria when judging, such as a sufficiently low stance, effective draw-back of the hip and clean athletic performance. The techniques shown under sport-oriented conditions no longer fulfilled their original purpose and became removed from the practical thinking behind the Kata of Okinawa.

It was, and is, nevertheless extremely important for the spread of Karate to further develop its character and role as a sport. Unfortunately, the various Karate associations have not been able to achieve consensus on a framework of rules for the sport. This is the reason why Karate has not yet been accepted into the Olympics. Judo and Tae Kwon Do have succeeded in attaining Olympic sport status. Of no lesser importance than Karate's sport character and worldwide presence, however, is knowledge of the particular uses of each single Kata. While Karate, and its Kata, now provide physical training for young people and adults, they contain

Evan Pantazi demonstrating a Kyusho Technique in floor combat, Grappling (Tegumi Waza)

the important element of self-defense, as well. In other words, the real intent has to be taken into account. It is easy to forget the elements of Tai Chi and Qigong which are hidden within the Kata.

Special breathing techniques go back to the training methods of China's Shaolin monasteries which were written down in secret documents, partly in Bubishi. The Kata's opening and closing movements, in particular, contain not only defensive aspects but also have a symbolic character such as the representation of Yin and Yang. Many of the positions in Karate Kata are related to those found in Tai Chi and Chi Gong. They serve the purpose of ensuring harmony and balance during training, as well as strengthening the Hara (Tandien) and stretching (and thereby activating) individual meridians. Gymnastics achieves much the same.

The Kata Kusanku, in fact, reveals that Sakugawa (1735) probably knew little about the cultural Chinese background. He used his knowledge of an old Okinawan fist-fighting method to modify this Kata (which he learned from the Chinese Delegate Ko Shu, 1756 A.D.) to be more combative. Another of Ko Shu Kun's students on Okinawa was more acquainted with the cultural background. Chatan Yara (1740-1812) and Kuniyoshi were able to pass on the more original version. Today's combat styles probably contain the Matsubayashi Ryu from Nagamine Shoshin (1907-1979), the original version of the Kata Kushanku, which is practiced in Shotokan as Kanku Dai and Kanku Sho. There is a responsibility still felt by the Okinawan Masters, to this day, to preserve and pass on the entire spectrum of Japan's unique cultural inheritance, in particular, that belonging to Okinawa.

3 The Three Levels of Karate Techniques:
Omote, Chuden and Okuden

Omote

A Karate student spends the first few years learning its technical particularities. This means learning correct execution of the movements to ensure the right body posture and building up speed and strength of technique. This applies equally to Kata training; primary importance is placed on the correct external form. The actual background of the Kata, its hidden applications (Okuden), is not taught to beginners at this stage. This does make the Kata less attractive for many students, particularly in the western world. On the surface, the various Kata do not seem to be appropriate for use in a realistic situation involving self-defense. It is difficult for a teacher at this "beginner" stage to infect his students with enthusiasm for the Kata. This was particularly problematic in the past, when generally only a few Kata were taught.

Okinawa's old Masters believed it necessary to practice only a few Kata, or sometimes just one, in order to perfect individual techniques and increase their effectiveness. They maintained that one single Master-Kata contained the entire repertoire for a realistic combative situation and for the required measure of self-defense. Today we know they were right. Yet it is understandable that a student might fail to appreciate the depth of the kata. The obvious techniques in the Kata are known in Japan as Omote. The variations in application due to individual differences are classified as Oyo Bunkai.

Tetsuhiro Hokama explained that the Kata in Karate can be compared to a large jug. Whereas a beginner and a student will only see the surface (and at best the bottom of the jug upon raising it), it is the Master (mostly from 3rd and 4th Dan) who enables an advanced student to view its core. Therefore, for an average student, the teachings of martial arts are mostly confined to the Omote – the obvious, easily recognized, simple techniques. Most students do not advance beyond the status of a beginner performing the Omote and their knowledge of the martial arts remains superficial.

Chuden

This refers to the techniques taught to a more experienced student at an intermediate level. They are more complex and can only be executed with a good deal of practice.

Okuden

The hidden, secret uses (Bunkai) of the Kata were passed on by the old Masters only to those students who had earned their complete trust. In Japan these techniques are described as Ura Waza. The secret techniques were also known as Okuden. As already mentioned, it is still common practice for those techniques which hold the true content of the Bunkai to be shown only to the higher Dans, and then only selectively. The passing on of advanced or hidden techniques is also carefully sifted. The particularly clever and refined techniques are only shown to especially trusted students (Uchi Deshi). The fact that Karate techniques belonging to the Okuden were not written down in earlier times makes it difficult to define the separate Kata, now, in the way they were probably defined 100 or 200 hundred years ago. Unfortunately, a lot of knowledge will remain hidden to us.

Oyo

Employing a Kata, however, need not remain confined to known techniques which have been passed down by word-of-mouth. Many Karate Masters have studied the techniques very closely and developed their own interpretations. These individual interpretations of a Kata are known as Oyo, and can distance themselves even further from the original Kata.

Although it is usually easy to recognize the most obvious uses (Omote), it is still often difficult to differentiate between Chuden, Okuden and Oyo.

Various methods are used to research the secret techniques of the Kata:

1. Comparative analysis of Parallel Kata

2. Analysis of related Kata

3. Tracing back to the Original-Kata (Koshiki Kata)

4. Analysis of similar patterns of movement

5. Decoding hidden techniques

6. Taking acupuncture into account with regard to sensitive body points (Kyusho)

7. Comparing Bunkai interpretations with rules taken from the " Bubishi" (plausibility check)

8. Viewing the versatility of one single technique in terms of Kyusho (sensitive points), Tuite (joint leverage) Shime Waza (throttling techniques) and Nage Waza (throwing techniques)

9. Checking the practicability of a Bunkai sequence. Can this interpretation also be applied in both "left" and "right" versions (for attacker and defender)?

10. Checking the practicability of a technique in a defensive situation. Reject what does not work.

With these methods we hope to rediscover important rules and movement patterns within the so-called coded Kata forms. We need to find the key before we can begin to translate the secret language of the Kata. We need to remember the acupuncture points of Chinese medicine when trying to recognize and analyze particular assault points in the Karate techniques of the Kata. Still, these methods cannot guarantee that we will rediscover and correctly interpret the versatility of the applications (Bunkai) which was so sought after and valued by the Masters of the past.

The following rules apply for a true Master-Kata:

1. There is more than one interpretation for a single Kata sequence.

2. There is no block in Karate; all techniques are an assault on sensitive body points and joints.

3. Each application must follow an overall strategy which is consistent with the individual Kata (given it represents the entire repertoire of one Master's combative art).

4. The techniques need not follow the fixed ordered sequence of the Kata. Each sequence should function as a separate technique within the segment.

5. The exercise must be successful against a persistent opponent.

6. Each technique must be capable of ending combat on its own (one strike, one blow).

7. Kata stances are not ballet, they need to be suited to the exercise (purpose).

8. Forwards movements are always attack; movements in retreat are not only defense.

9. Do not hang on a given Embusen (movement pattern), move as required by the situation.

10. There are no unnecessary movements in the Kata. Each movement has a deeper meaning and is absolutely economical. Combat does not allow for wasted time.

11. The backward movement of the hand to the hip comprises one application. It is not an end in itself nor merely a required part of a technique.

12. The Kata contains the correct angles of attack according to the rules of Kyusho.

13. Touching your own body in the Kata (Morote Uke) means attacking your opponent's body in the same place.

It is almost impossible to decode the hidden techniques visually or through literature. Instruction from an experienced Master and working together on analyzing the techniques within this framework is what will help to open Karate's inner soul. This is extremely difficult with Shotokan Karate, as the kata have been modified according to Qi Gong with the aim of promoting physical health. With this in mind, Gichin Funakoshi's remark: "Execute the Kata correctly, the actual fight is another matter" is clear for those in practice. Modification of a kata without the necessary background is falsification and leads to a distortion of Karate and the techniques lose their effectiveness and flexibility. This is, in fact, what the Old School Okinawan Masters say has happened thanks to modern Japanese styles.

Obviously, the rules of the Kata are very complex and not comprehensible for a beginner who is, by necessity, fully occupied in the first few years with external forms. According to Japanese tradition, one is only qualified to receive the Mekyo-Kaiden "permission to authentically pass on a Martial Art" after having achieved complete knowledge and full appreciation of the secret techniques (Okuden) of the Kata – which is understandable considering the complexity of the Kata. Furthermore, the Kata have been continually modified by various Masters, which makes it impossible to clearly differentiate between the different categories of Bunkai (Omote or Shoden/ lower level, Chuden and Okuden or Ura, and Oyo). We have no choice but to refer to either an obvious technique (Omote) or an advanced technique (Chuden to Okuden). This is where the greatest difficulty lies.

4 A Selection of Okinawan Masters

Most likely it was King Sho of Okinawa who around 1501 gave the decisive impulse for the development of Okinawan Karate with his law forbidding private possession of weapons and fighting with weapons. Yu Jianji (Kyoahagon Uekata Jikki, 1522) noted that the fighting spirit, usually seen among warriors, and the earnestness natural to the people of Okinawa, had been lost. Since weapons such as bows, swords, and spears were kept under lock and key in Shuri, he decided to breathe new life into the people by reactivating the art of combat without weapons, with just bare hands based on the old Okinawan Martial Arts. This was the actual beginning of Karate.

Kyoahagon was an ancestor of Tei Junsoku (Cheng Shunze). His father, in turn, was the second son of Hokama Chikudun Jitsubo, a fifth-generation descendant of Kyohagon Jikki. The name Karate (empty hand) appeared later, when Funakoshi (1868-1957) began to build up the popularity of Okinawa's Martial Arts on Japan's main island. A lot of terms were changed to cater to the Japanese ear. The original name, for example, was Tode Jutsu (Chinese Hand Martial Art). It was made up of Quan Fa (Kung Fu from the south of China), the Shorijin (Kempo) Ryu (from the north of China), China's Chin Na (grab hold and control), which later turned into Tuite Jutsu. On Okinawa Dim Mac (Dian Xue, combat utilizing sensitive acupuncture points) became Kyusho Jintai.

1   Zhen Hui (Jana Uekata Rizan) (1549-1611)

Jana came from a Diplomat Family in service of the Chinese Emperor. At the age of 16 he travelled to China where he studied under a Professor of the Ming Government. It was common in those days to see a lively exchange between Okinawa and China, aimed at expanding the culture of the Middle Kingdom on Okinawa. Jana continued to study the art of warfare, including Bujutsu, in China. After returning to Okinawa he instructed his students in Kume in Chinese Martial Arts. He was extremely successful and was held in such high esteem that he was given responsibility for the region of Ojana over Urasoe Magiri.

2   Kusanku (approx. 1700)

Kusanku is possibly one of the key figures in Okinawa's Karate. He was Military Attaché to the Chinese Emperor and arrived on Okinawa in 1756 with the Sappushi. Other well-known experts associated with the Sappushi (Delegates) were: Wanshu, Chinkan, Gankei, Passei and others. Even today, respective kata can be found (partially) under these names. Kusanku passed down one of the best known Kata under the same name. Sakugawa and Chatan Yara were two of his most famous students. The Tôde Master Sakugawa developed a more combative Kata called Sakugawa no Kushanku, while Chatan Yara developed a variation called Chatan Yara no Kushanku bearing a close relationship to the original Chinese form. As Chatan Yara had become intensely occupied with Chinese culture and had solid background knowledge, his Kata contained more elements of Tai Chi and Qi Gong. The Sakugawa Line gave rise to the different versions Kanku Dai and Kanku Sho, which are still practiced today in Shotokan Karate. The Chatan Yara Line can still be recognized on Okinawa in the Matsubayashi Ryu.

3   Chatan Yara (1740-1812)

Chatan Yara was a well-known Kobujutsu Master during the rule of King Sho Boku. Chatan Yara probably originally came from Shuri and was educated under the influence of the Chinese. He later moved to Chatan, which gave rise to his name: Yara of Chatan. He is the founder of the famous Kata Chatan Yara no Sai. He was greatly influenced by Wang Chung Yoh, an expert in Martial Arts.

4   Sakugawa Kanga (*1762-1843, or 1733-1815, or 1782-1837)
*No single definitive source

Sakugawa Tode (T. Hokama Museum)

Sakugawa came from Torihori (Akata) in Shuri. His original name was Teruya. Supposedly taught the Art of Chinese boxing (Tôde), among other things, by Master Iwah from China, he is also said to have been under the tutorship of the monk Takahara Peichin, and was sent to Peking several times. He changed his name after being awarded an Honor of Distinction (Chikudon Peichin) for Higher Service. He became acquainted with the Chinese Delegate and Martial Arts expert Kusanku (Ko Shu Kun) in Kume who taught him the Kata Kushanku, among others. He was a teacher at the Government School (Kogugaku) in the kingdom of Ikio. The Bujutsu-School Sakugawa no Kon, which later became famous, and the Kata bearing the same name can be attributed to him. His combat technique differed from the type of boxing already practiced on Okinawa, which originated in Fujian in the south of China. Sakugawa had an influence on Shuri Te, which was quite different than the Naha Te style from South China. He was also active in introducing Qigong and Chin Na to Okinawa.

The result was a blending of the Tôde, techniques for developing inner strength (Qigong) and the art of grabbing and joint rotation (Chin Na). His traditional Bo-Kata Sakugawa no Kon is quite famous. He is believed to have died in 1837 in Peking. He was already 78 years old when he taught Matsumura Sokon, who is supposed to have later found his remains in a cemetery outside Peking and returned them to Okinawa. Another of his students was Matsumora Kosaku (1829 to 1898), a well-known Master of Tomari Te.

5   Matsumura Sokon (1798-1890), Mrs Matsumura (Tsuru)

Matsumura was born in Yamakawa in Shuri. The information we have about him is not very exact. He was known as Bott Sho or Unyo. His Chinese name was Wu Chengda. He was in a relationship with a woman by the name of Tsuru, who also practiced the Martial Arts at a high level and is believed to have developed the

Matsumora Kosaku Monument in Naha.

Hangetsu Kata. He was taught Jigen Ryu (a Japanese style of sword fighting) by the Satsuma, and passed this knowledge on to several students such as Asato Anko (later Gichin Funakoshi's teacher) and Tarashiki Chochu. This was the start of the Tsuken Bo Kata, which was adopted by Tsuken Ueata Sesoku of Shuri and other students. He had a great influence on Kobudo.

Matsumura was responsible for establishing such important Karate rules as: "Move with the flow, victory by yielding, and the seven wisdoms of Karate."His many travels to the vicinity of Fouzhou, in China, allowed him to study Shaolin Kempo and armed techniques, which gave rise to his own particular style, the Shorin Ryu (or Shaolin Ryu). He was later appointed to the position of Head Bodyguard for the Ryu-Kyu King and received the honorary title of Bushi.

He took a copy of the "Bubishi" out of China, a document over China's Martial Arts which had long been held secret. One copy was kept under strict security by the Chinese families in Kume. The original is now possibly in Taiwan (according to verbal sources). It was in China that he became acquainted with Martial Arts through Master Iwah, who taught him the secret techniques of the Crane Style and the Hakatsuru Kata.

6   Matsumora Kosaku (1829-1898)

Matsumora Kosaku was a famous Tomari Te-Master. He was a strong fighter with a very direct character and joined up with his fellow citizens to protect his home town of Tomari from unwanted intruders. He had a naturally strong physique and was exceptionally talented. He studied under two teachers in Tomari: Uku Taryo and Teruya Kizo. A monument was erected in his honor in Tomari in May 1983. One of his many well-known students was Motobu Choki.

7   Itosu Anko (1828-1906, or 1829-1909)

Itosu Anko was born in Ishimine, Shuri. He is believed to have begun his training under Nagahama, although he is primarily seen as having been a student of Bushi Matsumora. Other influences played a role here, though, namely Ason's on Nagahama and Iwah's influence on Matsumura. Both Ason and Iwah were Sappushi bodyguards. Itosu Anko can be credited with doing a great deal to make Karate popular, introducing Karate into the school as a sport, and establishing the 10 Golden Rules of Karate. He made Karate simpler and developed the first curriculum for Karate education. His most important students were: Yabu Kentsu, Hanashiro Chomo, Funakoshi Gichin and Kyan Chotoku. He is believed to have been a very strong man of broad-shouldered stature.

8   Higaonna Kanryo (1853-1915)

Born in Naha, Nishi-Machi, he came from a family of warriors (Chiku Udun) which owned three small trading ships and so he, too, eventually arrived in the south of China. Higaonna began training as a young man under Arakaki Seisho. He later studied under Kojo Taitai, Wai Shinzan and Ru Ru Ko. He was heavily influenced by the Quanfa techniques of southern China and studied them in Fouzhou from 1876 to 1888. He taught a combination of two Chinese styles in his school in Naha, namely techniques from the Bai-he-quan (Crane Style) and Luo-han-quan (Shaolin Achat Boxing). He introduced a new form of the Sanchin Kata (with closed fists instead of the open hand). He taught many students who later went on to become quite famous, among

Higoanna Kanryo Monument, in the Foreground Tetsuhiro Hokama and Marc Kogel

them Miyagi Chojun. Higaonna is generally considered to be the one who systematized the typical Naha Te. (Miyagi renamed Higaonna's Naha Te, Goju Ryu, which means that today's Goju Ryu is actually the true Naha Te.) Of course, we still have to bear in mind that the "old" Naha Te already existed before Higaonna. Kyôda Kohatsu belonged to his inner student circle (Uchi deshi) and was introduced by him to the secret teachings of the "Bubishi" His student, Chôjun Miyagi, incorporated other influences from southern China and was later responsible for further development.

9   Funakoshi Gichin (1868 or 1870-1957)

There is conflicting information as to Funakoshi's date of birth, which we find explained in his book "Karate-Do, My Way of Life". His true date of birth was 1868, which fell in the EDO Period, the golden age of the Shoguns. To be able to register himself for Studies of Medicine in Tokyo, however, he had to change his date of birth to 1870 (Meiji-Period) in order to be eligible to sit for the entrance exam. He came from ordinary Okinawan stock, overshadowed by the problems accompanying an alcoholic father.

Funakoshi was, in his own words, a rather weak child and it was his training in Karate which improved both his constitution and his health. He trained under numerous well-known Masters, including: Kiyuna, who could peel the bark off a tree with his bare hands in a flash, Master Toonno of Naha (an acknowledged teacher of Confucius), Master Niigaki, Master Matsumura and Master Azato. Azato introduced Funakoshi to his friend, Itosu Anko. Funakoshi, as a result, became a student of the famous Itosu Anko. He profited greatly from this Master's systematic approach and also apparently learned the secrets of the Bubishi. Funakoshi was not accepted as a Medical Student and so he ended up becoming a teacher at the age of 18.

In 1922 he travelled to Tokyo to demonstrate Okinawa's Martial Arts at a presentation in Ochanomizu. Karate Clubs were established at Keio, Takshoku and Waseda Universities. The Shotokan Dojo was built in Tokyo in 1939, bearing his pseudonym "Shoto". He had changed the face of Okinawa's Martial Arts, enabling them to make greater inroads as a sport in schools and at the universities. Jigoro Kano, Judo's founder, was a great inspiration to him. This later gave rise to the very successful JKA (Japanese Karate Association).

Funakoshi wrote numerous books which promoted Karate throughout the world. In one book he laid down the 20 guiding principles which go back to the teachings of the "Bubishi." A memorial in his honor was erected on Okinawa 50 years after his death to commemorate his role in helping Karate to achieve worldwide recognition.

10 Motobu Choki (1870-1944)

Choki Motobu was born in Akahira (Shuri) as the third son of Motobu Udun (Anji), an Okinawan Lord, 6th son of the King of Okinawa (Sho Shitsu 1629-1668). As a child he was commonly known as Saburo. Being third in the line of descent, he had no claims to privileged education or to specialized training in the particular combative arts of the family Udundi. It was his own consuming interest in the Martial Arts which led Motobu to practice what he had secretly observed. He gathered experience in the street fights that often erupted, particularly in red-light districts. His daredevil nature made it difficult to find a suitable teacher. Tokumine Peichin became his first teacher, though he was known as a drinker lacking in self-control. Motobu was, however, finally able to find acknowledged Karate teachers

Motobu Choki (in the T. Hokama Museum)

who agreed to help him: Sokon Matsumura, Anko Itosu and Kosaku Matsumora, to name just three. Motobu was extremely agile, which led to him being nicknamed Saru or Shinpan, Motobu the Monkey. He had a reputation as a strong and uncompromising fighter.

His venture of a horse-taxi on Okinawa failed and he went on to Osaka to work as a night watchman. He had some spectacular successes in exhibition fights in Osaka. His knock out triumph over a foreign boxer led to an article about him in "King" magazine, in which a photograph of Funakoshi was mistakenly printed, unfortunately.

Nevertheless, the article boosted Karate's image and popularity in Japan. Funakoshi was heavily criticized by Choki Motobu for softening Karate by re-implementing it as a Sport, which had the effect of significantly changing Okinawa's old Martial Arts.

Motobu released two books: "Okinawa Kempo Karate Jutsu, Kumite-hen" (1926) and "Watashi no Karate-Jutsu" (1932). Matsumora taught him the Kata Bassai and Naihanchi, the latter building the basis of his own special combative system. In

1927 he was involved in founding the Karate-Jutsu Kenkyukai at Tokyo University. In 1934 he opened his Dadokan Dojo in Esamachi, Tokyo. He later returned to Okinawa and died a few years later in 1944. He left behind a number of renowned students, including Nagamine Sochin and Ohtsuka Hironori. Typical for his style of fighting is the high base stance, a striving for close-combat distancing, the key position Kiba Dachi, uncompromisingly simple techniques and using defense to attack. His style, Motobu- Ryu Kempo-Karate, must not be confused with "Motobu Udundi" which is the particular style belonging to the Motobu family and comparable to Aikijutsu. One representative of this style was Uehara Seikishi (Okinawa). Choki Motobu's son, Chosei, has been designated at his successor and chosen to spread his particular style of combat.

I I Uechi Kanbun (1877-1948)

Uechi Kanbun was born on May 5, 1877, in the city of Motobu on a peninsula in the north of Okinawa. The family had decided to go into retreat to escape the harassment from the Satsuma Clan. He fled to China in 1897 to avoid having to do military duty in Japan. In Fuzhou he was taught southern Shaolin Tiger Boxing by Shu Shiwa. He left his first Master's Dojo for personal reasons and joined up with Chou Tsu-Ho (Zhou Zi-He), a monk who taught him the Martial Arts of Pangai-Nun and herbal medicine. He later opened his own Elementary Martial Arts School, which unfortunately came to have a poor reputation (due to clashes between his students and the general public) leading to his return to Okinawa in 1910.

Having refused military service, he had to go into hiding but on being recognized he moved to Japan's main island in 1921. Disappointment had, more than once, caused him to break off developing his combative talents. He opened a Dojo in Nakayama in 1926, which was named Pangai Noon-Ryu Karate-Jutsu of the Kenkyu-jo in 1932. It became known as Uechi-Ryu in 1940. His style confined itself to the Sanchin, Seisan and Sanseriu Kata and later included Sanchin and Tensho (both open handed). He had several outstanding students, one of these being his son Uechi Kanei (1911-1991), who continued to follow in his father's footsteps. He returned to Izumi on Okinawa in 1910.

I2 Wu Hsienhui (Go Kenki, Wu Xian Gui, Yoshikawa 1886-1940)

Wu Hsienhui moved from Fujian to Okinawa in 1912, at the age of 26. He had a tea business in Higashi-Machi, was acquainted with quite a few Goju Ryu people and taught several students. Among these was his friend, Uechi Kanbun (whom he considered to be particularly gifted), as well as Miyagi Chojun, Shinpo Matayoshi, Mabuni Kenwa and Kyoda Juhatsu. He taught the Crane Style of Nepai (Chinese:

Nipaipo, Japanese Niju Hachi Ho; the same description still exists for an old Kata of 28 Steps). His style, which contained a lot of toughening-up techniques, was known as Kingai Ryu. He travelled to China with Miyagi Chojun to get to know Higoanna Kanryu teacher. He propagated the following Kata: Nipaipo (Niju Hachi Ho), Paipuren (Happoren), Hakudo, Hakufa (Hakutsuru), Hakutsuru no Te (White Crane Hand), Sanchin and possibly Wanshu. These made up part of what he taught to his students Kyoda Juhats and Mabuni Kenwa.

The White Crane Style can be found in his Kata, Hakutsuru. It is considered to be one of the elementary forms of Karate. Other students of interest were Uechi Kunbun, Miyagi Chojun and Shinpo Matayoshi. In Shanghai he brought together Miyagi Chojun and the famed Miao Xing (1881-1939), who taught the Monkey Fist style of Qua Fa (Luoha Quan). This probably makes Go Kenki one of the most important teachers of Okinawan Karate. He was successful in bringing a copy of Bubishi to Okinawa and was instrumental in explaining it and traditional Chinese medicine as well.

13   Matayoshi Shinko (1888-1947)

Born in Kakinihana, Naha, he grew up in Shinbaru, Chatan and became interested as a child in the weapons of the Bo, Ecu, Kama and Sai. He learned their uses from Higa of Gushikawa Tairagawa. He learned the Art of the Tonfa and the Nunchaku from Ire (Jitode-moushi-gwa) of Nosata. At the end of the Meiji Era he went to Manchuria in northern China and joined up with mountain bandits who taught him to ride, throw a lasso, shoot with a bow and arrow, and Shuriken Jutsu. He returned to Okinawa temporarily and held public performances in Osaka, Tokyo and Kyoto with other practicing Martial Arts experts such as Funakoshi Gichin, Mabuni Kenwa and Motobu Choki. He then travelled back to Shanghai to study Tinbe, Suruchin and Nunti Bo, and traditional Chinese medicine, acupuncture and moxibustion from Master Jin Ying (Kingai). In southern China he also learned Kingainoon (Hakatsuru-Ken), i.e. the Crane Fist Style. His broad education and extensive knowledge assured him a reputation of note on his return to Okinawa. He was followed by his son, Shinpo Matayoshi, who founded the All Okinawan Kobudo Federation.

14   Miyagi Chojun (1888-1953)

Chojun Miyagi was born on April 25, 1888, in Naha, Higashi-Machi. He was the third son of a family of Okinawa's aristocracy (Kakyu-Shizoku). The family was wealthy and owned trading ships and a business which imported herbal medicines from China, among other things. His father died early and Miyagi Chojun inherited his fortune at the young age of 5 years. With the support of his family he was able

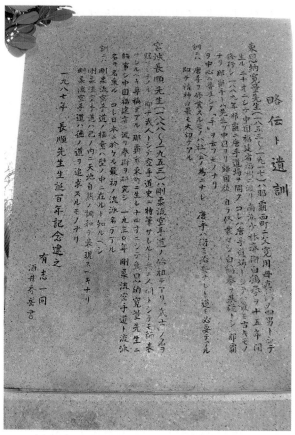

Memorial to Chojun Miyagi on Okinawa

to begin learning the Martial Arts at an early age. His first teacher was Master Aragaki Ryuko. In 1902 he introduced Miyagi, then aged 14, to Master Higashionna Kanryo. From this point on Miyagi became Kanryo's student. After the death of his teacher in 1916, Chojun Miyagi followed his example by travelling to China to study the Martial Arts. He was in Fujian in 1915 and then in Shanghai in 1936 with the aim of doing research on Chinese Boxing from the south of China. In 1929 he began to bring more of a system into the training with the incorporation of preparatory strengthening exercise, supplementary training methods, elementary schooling and concluding exercises. This gave Karate the additional aspect of physical education. Although he had learned the Sanchin Kata in its original form, he modified it to become much harder with the aim of steeling the body through special Qigong breathing techniques.

He supplemented it with his Tensho Kata which basically contained elements of the White Crane Kata. During the early Showa Period he taught in police schools, colleges and at the Naha School of Commerce, and later at Kanzei University. He was instrumental in the spread of Karate on Japan's main island with performances on Okinawa for the Japanese Emperor as well as for Judo visitors from Osaka and Tokyo. He was a member of the Dai Nippon Butokukai. Under pressure to define his Karate style, he chose the name Goju Ryu, Go meaning hard and Ju meaning soft. His inspiration for the name came from an excerpt from the Bubishi which says: "Everything in and throughout the universe breathes hard and soft." He maintained a friendly relationship with Jigoro Kano. He created two kata to improve Karate instruction in schools: Gekisai Dai Ich and Gekisai Dai Ni, which can be compared to the Heian Kata in Shotokan Karate.

Chojun Miyagi died of heart problems in 1953 at a relatively young age. A successor had unfortunately not been appointed, which resulted in a good deal of conflict among his students. The question of Chojun Miyagi's true inheritor has still not been solved. His best student, Shinzato Jinan, was killed during an American attack in World War II. His Goju Ryu has been passed on by his students Seiko Higa and Miyazato Eiichi, and through Gogen Yamagushi on Japan's main island.

15   Mabuni Kenwa (1898-1952)

Mabuni Kenwa was a descendant of the warrior, Oni Ufugusuku Kenyu, and the Founder of the Shito-Ryu. He was born in Shuri and was a small and sickly child. He studied under various Masters such as Itosu Anko, Higaonna Kanryo, Arakaki Seisho and Bushi Tawada. He studied the Shurite, the Naha Te and the Yamani Ryu under Oshiro.

He worked as a police official and taught Karate in Shuri. Considering the rather poor outlook for the future on Okinawa, it was not difficult for him to be motivated to a move to Japan's main island by Kano during a Judoka demonstration he had organized. He started up a Dojo in Osaka and created his own style, which was characterized by an enormous variety of style elements and different Kata. He also taught at Kansei University and at Tokyo University. It did not take him long to develop protective clothing in order to better try out the techniques in full. According to the experts, he is probably the only person at the time that had a complete overview of both the Shuri Te and the Naha Te. The name Shito Ryu is composed of the first syllables of the names of his teachers Itosu and Higaonna. He published two papers, "Seipei Kenkyu" and "Karate Do Nyumon". He died on May 23, 1952.

16   Soken Hohan (1891-1982)

Soken Hohan was born on May 25, 1891 in the city of Nishihara on Okinawa. He was a great-grandson of the famous Bushi Matsumura Sokon. His uncle, Nabe Matsumura, taught him the secret familial Martial Arts and the Tonfa Jutsu. In addition, he studied Sai and Kama. He learned Bojutsu and Nunchaku from Komesu. Hohan founded the orthodox Matsumura style (Shorin- Ryu Matsumura Seito). He was a significant influence on many famous students and played an important role in understanding the Kyusho Jintai.

17   Tomoyose Ryuyu (1897-1970)

Tomoyose Ryuyu's research work on the martial arts led to him being declared a protected living cultural asset. He studied under Uechii Kanbun in Wakayama and trained with Akamine Kanei. He is the author of a book called "Kenpo Karate-Jutsu Hiden" in which he concentrated on strikes to vital points and traditional Chinese medicine.

His research work was based on the so-called "Bubishi". He also did additional research on circadian rhythms and its bearing on the treatment of injuries. He died of an acute illness in 1970 at a relatively young age.

18   Taira Shinken (1897-1970)

Taira Shinken was born on June 12, 1897, on the Island of Kumejima, his original name being Maesato. He trained under Gichin Funakoshi in Tokyo, and under Mabuni Kenwa. He studied Kobujutsu under Yabiku Moden and started up his first Shotokan Dojo in Ikaho Onsen, in the province of Gunma. Relatively little Kobudo

Taira Shinken, above left (T. Hokama Karate Museum)

was practiced on Okinawa at this time, and Taira Shinken became intensely involved with reviving it. In 1959 he opened a Kobujutsu Dojo in Naha. He is Founder of the Ryu Kyu Kobudo Hozon Shinkokai Organization.

He spent his entire life engaged in research on Kobudo. When he died of cancer in 1970, he was succeeded by his student Akamine Eisuke. He was survived by many well-known students, such as Inoue Motokatsu, Hayashi Teruo, Mabuni Kenwa and others.

19   Higa Seiko (1898-1966)

He was born on November 18, 1898 in Higashi-Machi in Naha and began his Karate training under Higaoanna Kanryo at the age of 13. Following Higaonna's death, he continued to train with his student Chojun Miyagi in 1915. In 1919 he was appointed substitute teacher at a primary school. He put an end to his career as a teacher in 1920 and became a policeman. The prospect, however, of being transferred north caused him to resign and in 1933 he started up a Dojo in Shimoizumi in Naha.

Responsibility for the Kobudo in the Dojo was delegated to Matayoshi Shinpo. The Dojo changed its location over the years. In 1937 he moved to Saipan and opened a Dojo there. He returned to Okinawa in 1937 and started up another Dojo in 1947 in Itoman in the south of Okinawa. In 1956 he was elected Vice President of the Goju-Ryu Shinkokai Organization, following the deaths of Joule and Miyagi. Miyagi`s students gave him the title "Hanshi". In 1956 he also became Vice President of the Okinawan Karate Do Federation, together with Nagamine Shoshin, and supported its President, Chibana Choshin. In 1960 he became this Organization's second President, after which he founded the International Karate Kobudo Federation. In 1960 he also opened a Dojo with the name of Shodokan. He is considered to be one of the most capable teachers of Karate and Goju Ryu.

20   Tokuyama Seiken (1900-1958)

Tokuyama was born in Yamakawa in Shuri. The famous Kobudo Master Oshiro Chojo lived in his neighborhood and so he began his Karate and Kobudo training with him while he was still young. He later worked as a policeman. Despite not being tall, he specialized in kicking out of the jump. He was slim, extremely strong and also so fast that he could catch an Okinawan Habu, a venomous pit viper, with a thin bamboo stick. According to Tetsuhiro Hokama, his grandson, he was also able to grab rats in a dark room in his sleep. Tokuyama handed down many different Kobudo Kata such as Chibana no Sai, Goeku no Ekudi, Kama no Ti and Tokuyama no Tunfa, for example.

21 Nagamine Shoshin (1907-1997)

Nagamine Shoshin began Karate training under Chibana Choshin at the age of 17. At 19 he became a student of Arakaki Ankichi and studied Shuri Te. He started training with Arakaki Ankichi's student, Kyan Chotoku, at 26. He was 31 and studying at the Police Academy in Tokyo when he learned Tomari Te from Motobu Choki. He was stationed in Kadena between 1931 and 1935 and started studying Kendo during this time. He was awarded the Renshi title by the Dai in Nippon Butokukai in 1940. In 1956 he was appointed Vice President of the Okinawan Karate Do Federation and, in 1967, was elected President of the All Okinawan Karate Do Federation. He published several books in English and was particularly committed to the spread of Karate, especially his own style known as Matsubayashi Ryu. He was in charge of 30 Dojos in Japan, 40 in the USA and more in many other countries.

22 Uechi Kanei (1911-1991)

He was born on June 26, 1911, in Motobu, the son of Uechi Kanbun, Founder of Uechi Ryu. It was he who further modernized his father's Karate. He added five more kata to the 3 basic kata: Sanchin, Seisan and Sanseru, without distorting or falsifying their direction in style. He also created special Kumite forms and developed the warm-up exercises further. He is credited with establishing the world famous All Okinawan Karate Do Championships.

23 Fukuchi Seiko (1919-1975)

Fukuchi was born in Nishi Shin-Machi in Naha. He trained in the Dojo operated by Higa Seiko. During his military service with the Japanese Army in Peking from 1940 to 1943, he learned Chinese Boxing. Initially he was Chairman of the Karate Department of the Association for Physical Education in Okinawa and later became Head of this Organization in May 1948. In 1968 he was appointed Director of the Old Okinawan Goju-Kai. He travelled to Tokyo with other Karate Masters to give presentations of Okinawan Karate. He was a pragmatic Karate teacher with clearly defined principles such as "attack and defense are one and the same" or "always be ready to take the initiative, even when your opponent is first to attack." Unfortunately, he died much too early, as the result of a stroke.

24 Matayoshi Shinpo (1921-1997)

Born on December 27, 1921 in Kina (a suburb of Yomitan), he was the son of the famous Kobudo Master Shinko Matayoshi. He began training with his father at the age of 7. He later became interested in Shorin Ryu Karate and studied it under Kyan

Chotoku. In 1938 he learned the southern style of Shaolin Boxing and the Crane Style from Go Kenki. He was particularly active in promoting the spread of Kobudo both nationally and abroad and built up a world-wide reputation in Kobudo. He founded the Ryu-Kyu Kobudo Renmei, which was later renamed Zen Okinawan Kobudo Renmei. His students continue to travel the world to further promote the spread of Okinawan Kobudo.

Matayoshi Shinpo, right, and Tetsuhiro Hokama 1965 in Seiko Higa's Dojo

5 Fifty Years of Okinawan Karate

By Tetsuhiro Hokama

Chojun Miyagi wrote in his final years: "What is Karate? It has no weapons and in times of peace it should not be used the way it was originally intended but rather for the training of character and attitude. In the face of lawlessness, however, it can be used for self-defense. There are many situations in which one can use Karate to repel an attacker with just the use of the body." He also wrote: "Do not strike others and do not allow yourself to be struck. The real aim is to not become involved in a confrontation at all." It is easy to see that Miyagi had internalized the philosophy behind Karate very well.

Itoso Anko and his student Funakoshi Gichin also stated: "There is no first strike in Karate." It is a well-known fact that both of them promoted Karate as a Martial Art for gentlemen.These days Karate no longer belongs to Okinawa or Japan alone. In fact, it is much more popular overseas than in its country of origin. It is estimated that a total of 40 million people practice Karate in over 140 countries throughout the world. Can any other of Japan's cultural assets claim such a huge number of enthusiasts? Although Karate's roots are to be found in China, it was on Okinawa that it developed and spread further under the name of Karate Do. Bearing this in mind, the old Ti Art of Self-Defense has expanded so much that even Karate masters, myself included, cannot explain it completely. During my teaching and practice of Karate and Kobudo in more than 22 countries I strive to achieve the ultimate in performing these Martial Arts and consider myself privileged to know the significance of Okinawan Karate as an art which can be practiced over an entire lifetime.

Karate has always been seen in Okinawa not only as a combative skill but also as a cultural heritage and an essential part of daily life. This makes it easier to understand that new local cultural forces and circumstances made change in Karate inevitable the moment it was transplanted to another country.

An analogy can be made with traditional cooking. When we talk about importing original Chinese or French cooking to Japan, this does not necessarily mean that typical Japanese ingredients or cooking techniques are not used so much as that they are slightly modified to suit local needs and tastes. A committed traditionalist would, of course, refuse to describe these dishes as typically Chinese or French unless they are exactly the same as the original.

Having transferred the art of Karate and Kobudo from China to the Ryu Kyu Islands, its Masters were able to maintain it in its authentic form for quite some time. Once it had taken root in its new homeland, however, it became increasingly influenced by Okinawa's own particular culture. The introduction of Karate into

Okinawa's school system meant that some of the Kata had to be modified to make them suitable for teaching in schools. There are, however, numerous current movements on Okinawa which concern themselves with maintaining the true classical forms.

At the time of its introduction to Japan's main island in 1920, Karate was taught in its original form. Over time it changed more and more to incorporate Japanese characteristics. The names of the Kata were changed and the techniques altered. Further information on the history of Karate can be found in other books published by the author.

The Martial Arts of Japan have always followed a different path to the spirit and the techniques of the Ryu Kyu Island's Martial Arts. Nevertheless, Okinawan Karate has had a decisive effect on the overall development of the Japanese tradition. Karate's arrival in the USA and the rest of the world began in 1950. Fifty years later this style of combat is known worldwide. Now, at the start of the 21st century, we are occupied with rediscovering the unique history of these combative skills.

Having arrived in the USA, Karate was influenced by local cultural aspects and by the mentality and attitude of the active American Karatekas. It became more dynamic under the influence of boxing and other sports. It moved away from its spiritual element towards a more aggressive interpretation in line with the American firearms culture.

Okinawan Karate Do is similar to the traditional dances of the Ryu Kyu Islands. The center of gravity is shifted downwards and inward. Suddenly we see the introduction of kicks above the waistline. Numerous kicking techniques were exported to Okinawa from other countries such as Korea, and then incorporated into the traditional techniques. This development is basically a result of the influence of the "new" aspects of sport and competition.

Karate's arrival in Europe resulted in the same process as in the USA – it was influenced by European Martial Arts. The same applies to Kobudo. We must understand that a weapon itself provides the impulse for defending oneself against it. For example, the shield provides protection against the sword. Weapons were developed in Japan as a means of defense against the sword. Okinawa has no natural reserves of iron, meaning that its culture was based on weapons and tools made of wood. Most of the Kobudo weapons are therefore wooden, e.g. Bo, Tonfa, Eku and Nunchaku. Europe, on the other hand, had a stone-age and an iron-age, so that ships and firearms were developed at an early stage.

It was natural for Karate and Kobudo to have always developed along the lines of the cultural characteristics of the respective host country. With their Chinese origin, the Martial Arts were accompanied by techniques for acupuncture, meridian theory and the secrets of the sensitive and vital body points as well as boxing. This style of combat was modified on the Ryu Kyu Islands to become that which we now know as Karate Do. Following its arrival on the Japanese Main Island, Karate quickly became very popular as a sport and for open competition. Overseas, more and more importance was given to the aspect of sport. Nowadays, the competitive side of the sport has largely taken over in offshore countries. It is impossible to ignore the fact that a wide gap has formed between these techniques and the classical techniques of Karate. Fortunately, the Karate, which originally came out of Okinawa, has not been completely affected by these same changes. Nevertheless, it is surprising to see what has happened to the "old" Karate in other countries overseas.

Who is referring to whom? Although similar, overseas Karate still differs greatly from the original. The author believes that the original Karate Do may have no future if we neglect to reflect on the classical methods of the Ryu Kyu Islands.

We do see a movement throughout the world to rediscover the roots and traditions of Karate Do. Hopefully, the future creative development of Karate Do will take these traditions into account with full awareness of the importance of their classical and historical aspects. This is the true meaning behind the words: On Ko Chin Shin (Wholeness of mind, body, and elementary strength). We cannot talk about Karate Do without relating it to Okinawa's history. And it is always the central thread which is important in history. Although my research on the subject is not yet completed, I feel it is a "must" to write a book on the subject.

It was no great difficulty for me to gather material, considering that I run a Karate Museum. However, in putting the material together, it became obvious that there are many gaps in the period before World War II. At first, an incomplete book seemed out of the question and the project was nearly abandoned. However, I realized how important it is to just put together as much historical information as possible, even when this represents only a part of the total picture. This is not only vital as a foundation for future research, but is also helpful to give modern Karatekas at least an impression of this very special history. Accepting that there may be a few errors or omissions, I decided to document as much history as possible.

I hope to have motivated you to become active and make suggestions as to how to supplement this work to achieve an even more objective level.

If this publication helps to increase the appreciation of the culture of Karate even a little, then we have fulfilled a very major aim. (Hokama Tetsuhiro, January 21, 2001).

Dr. Tetsuhiro Hokama in his Karate Museum in Nishihara Okinawa

Comment of H. Kogel: We currently see a satisfying trend toward an ever increasing number of Budo enthusiasts, who are learning the traditional methods of the old Martial Arts. It is important to continue to study the Martial Arts after the competitive phase of youth. There is so much content in the Martial Arts which should be studied over one's entire lifetime and which needs to be spiritually and physically absorbed. Okinawa's old combative skills cannot be limited to competition; the aesthetic appearance of a Kata is not of critical importance. Rather, it is important to know what lies hidden in its use. In my experience, what is often officially described as Bunkai (Omote) is completely unfounded. What is often quoted as the secret techniques of Karate (Okuden) are revealed only when one devotes himself thoroughly to the subject, i.e. one understands Tuite and Kyusho techniques and finds a key to translating the secret language of the Kata. Deciphering the coded old traditional Karate Kata is extremely difficult and involves a tremendous amount of work. It is well worth the effort, however, to involve oneself with this facet of Karate.

6   Karate as Seen by Today's Okinawan Grand Masters

Okinawa remains the birthplace of an old combative art which largely emerged from Chinese systems such as Quan Fa (from the southern Chinese province of Fujian) and Shaolin Kempo (from the mountains north of Beijng), as well as from Okinawa's fist fighting system, Okinawan Te. The following comments are based on an interview which took place between the authors and Karate Grand Masters representing differing styles on Okinawa. Basically the interview centered on their attitude toward Karate and how it differs from the Martial Arts of the main Japanese island and China. Tetsuhiro Hokama, 10th Dan Karate, Kobudo and Kyusho Jutsu Hanshi (who is also an Historian), arranged the interviews, accompanied us on our visits to the Grand Masters and translated from Japanese into English so that we could fully understand the statements of these Karate Grand Masters.

Comments by Isao Shima, 10th Dan Karate Hanshi, 10th Dan Kobudo Hanshi (70 years old), President of the Okinawan Karate- Kobudo Federation, Shorin Ryu (Matsubayashi) Karate Do

Isao Shima is an exponent of Shorin Ryu (Matsubayashi Ryu) and was personally one of Nagamine Shoshin's students. He is a former School Director and practiced Karate intensively parallel to his job. As many Grand Masters do, he has a Dojo which is located at his home. He believes that Okinawa occupies a special place when it comes to Karate. He sees it as the very cradle of Karate and as Karate's

From left to right Marc Kogel (3rd Dan Karate, 1st Dan Bo-Jutsu), Tetsuhiro Hokama (10th Dan Karate/Kobudo Hanshi), Isao Shima (10th Dan Karate/Kobudo Hanshi), Prof. Dr. Helmut Kogel (6th Dan Karate/5th Dan Kobudo Renshi)

Mecca for Karatekas interested in researching its roots. Karate is a fixed part of Okinawa's culture. A meeting took place on the day following our interview on January 11, 2007, which was attended by the Ministry for Culture, Isao Shima, several other Karate Grand Masters and the University. The purpose of this meeting was the development of a new program to coordinate and combine efforts between those actively advancing the interests and importance of Karate and those working to make the island more attractive for tourists. Obviously foreign Karatekas are an important group of tourists and new programs should make Okinawa even more interesting to them. As a result, committees have been established at the University for researching Karate's history and techniques. The basic difference between Karate on Okinawa and on the main island of Japan is that in the former it is seen as part of the island's culture whereas on Japan's main island it is generally sport- and competition oriented. Shima considers both aspects to be important and believes both sides need to be intensively promoted.

A fundamental component of Karate is "Shin Gi Tai" (harmony of body and mind). There are principles firmly rooted in the rules of the "Bubishi" which are contained in Funakoshi's 20 guidelines of Karate. Related guidelines can be found in principles laid down by other pioneers of Karate, such as Chojun Miyagi, for example. Of no little importance are a well-balanced and peace-seeking character and staying power which should apply to one's working and family life. Personal reliability and trustworthiness are also very important. The much quoted secrets and secret techniques of Karate and its special Kata were also a topic for discussion. In Shima's opinion, despite the dangers that accompany passing on secret techniques to Karatekas outside Japan (such as change or even falsification), it also offers an opportunity for further development and new impulses. Since humans vary in their physique, patterns of movement, character, culture, etc., Karatekas from different nations are naturally going to cause changes in interpretation and practice. Shima sees this as advantageous for Karate's future development, and believes teachers of Karate must take these aspects into consideration when dealing with their students. Obviously, not all budding Karatekas can be treated in the same way, especially in view of differences in their stamina. It is not possible for a Karate teacher to draw out each and every desirable characteristic from his students. Each person is ultimately responsible for himself. Understandably there will always be a number of Karate students who do not continue with their Karate training beyond a certain point. This is something over which the Karate teacher has only a limited amount of influence.

Sensei Shima also stated his position regarding various Karate styles. He sees the actual distance between opponents as one important difference between Goju Ryu and styles related to Shorin Ryu. Shorin Ryu is comprised of numerous techniques suitable for more distanced combat, whereas in Goju Ryu one will find many techniques intended for fighting at close range. Okinawan Karate is rooted in Okinawa Te, an old fist fighting style, and China's Martial Arts such as Shorinji Kempo and Quanfa. Despite their common origins, China's Martial Arts and Okinawa's Karate and Kobudo followed a different path in their development. The Chinese combative styles concentrated on developing a more elegant, acrobatic style whereas the art of Okinawa's Karate is more practical. The terms Okinawan Te, Karate Jutsu, Tote Jutsu, Tuite Jutsu and Kyusho Jutsu are often interpreted in the western world in a contradictory way. Okinawa's Grand Masters see Okinawan Te as the old fist fighting art of Okinawa. Tote (Toudi) Jutsu is the so-called Chinese Hand and Karate Jutsu refers to the combative system which evolved out of Okinawan Te and the Chinese style of Tote Jutsu. Tuite Jutsu arose out of the Chinese art of Chin Na (grab and pin down, i.e. control). Kyusho Jutsu came from China's Dim Mac and incorporates knowledge and use of the body's sensitive points, which is closely connected to acupuncture.

Another interview was conducted with Nakamura Yoshio, an honorable 90 year old Master of Shuri Te. He allowed us to use one of the books he had written, which contained descriptions of all Shuri Te Kata (which are closely related to the Shotokan Kata). Some of the analyses in this volume were put together with the help of his monograph. The common roots of Shotokan Karate and Shuri Te became

obvious in the Kata book. A well-known Shuri Te Master of the past was Itosu Anko (1830-1915) who, among other things, taught Gichin Funakoshi (1868 or 1870-1957). The analysis of Nakamura's Shuri Te book also shows, beyond a doubt, the changes which had later been made by Funakoshi.

Comments made by Nakamura Yoshio, 10th Dan Karate Hanshi, Councillor Shuri Te (90 years old)

Sensei Nakamura is a supporter of the old traditional school of Okinawan Karate. Makiwara Training is every bit as important to him as action arising out of movement. In his youth he

Nakamura Yoshio 10th Dan Karate Hanshi

trained three hours a day. He believes it strengthens the bones, which is important and indispensable for effective Karate.

He considers a firm hold to be an absolute necessity in this Martial Art. It needs to be taught, strengthened and reinforced by special training methods such as Chin Na. A large number of opponents challenged him in his youth and visited his Dojo for this purpose. The stronger he became, the fewer challenges he had. In his opinion, the primary purpose

Nakamura (Shuri Te), right, in younger years, left Go Kenki (Wu Hsienhui 1886-1940), Master of the White Crane Style

of an advanced level of Karate is not combat, but following the aims of the "Bubishi", and Funakoshi's 20 principles. This endows Karate with value for one's entire life.

Sanchin Kata, Breaking Test in Tetsuhiro Hokama's Dojo

Funakoshi's 20 principles:

1. Do not forget that Karate begins and also ends with a bow.

2. There is no first strike in Karate.

3. Karate stands on the side of justice.

4. Get to know yourself first, then others.

5. Mentality over technique.

6. First, make your mind free.

7. Calamity springs from carelessness.

8. Karate extends beyond the Dojo.

9. Karate is a lifelong pursuit.

10. Apply the way of Karate to all things in life. This is its beauty.

11. Karate is like boiling water: without heat it returns to its tepid state.

12. Do not think of winning, but of not losing.

13. Adjust your assessment of your opponent.

14. The outcome of a fight depends on how one deals with emptiness and fullness (weakness and strength).

15. Think of your opponent's hands and feet as swords.

16. If you look beyond your own horizons, you will discover a million enemies.

17. Kamae (ready stance) is for beginners, one later stands in Shizentai (natural stance).

18. Perform the Kata precisely; the fight itself is another matter.

19. Do not forget withdrawal of power, the extension and contraction of the body, the speed or slowness of the technique.

20. Always be mindful, diligent and resourceful in following your pursuit of the Way.

A visit was also paid to Grand Master Jyosei Yogi, who practices Kounan Ryu, a form of Uechi Ryu. In recent years, Uechi Ryu has been split into many different categories. Its origins go back to the old, Chinese Pangai Nun. Master Yogi is a particularly open and friendly person, who also placed emphasis on the special role of Shin Gi Tai (harmony of body and mind).

Comments made by Jyosei Yogi, 8th Dan Karate Kyoshi, 8th Dan Kobudo Kyoshi, Executive Adviser Okinawan Kobudo Rensei-Kai, Kounanryu Karate Dojo (73 years old).

For Jyosei Yogi the most important thing in Karate is the heart, i.e. inner attitude. When it comes to the spread

Jyosei Yogi 8th Dan Karate/Kobudo Kyoshi

of Karate, he holds the same opinion as Master Shima. He sees no future in keeping Karate to oneself and hiding its secrets, as was usually the case in Okinawa in times past. He stresses the importance of spreading Karate throughout the world so that it can develop further.

He, too, sees Okinawan Karate as traditionally-oriented and practical in its training and implementation whereas the practice of Karate on Japan's main island has the character of a sport. He believes both facets to be of equal importance. Karate will always be subject to change when practiced in different countries.

Each and every Master teaches differently, just as each and every student develops differently. This means that Karate Do will always change with them. Karate Do also exists outside the Dojos. It trains body and mind, and provides us with experience for life as a family member and in our work place.

Karate gives us tactical guidelines and rules, teaches good behavior and helps to create understanding between individuals. It ensures more harmony in relationships and can be instrumental in aiding peace. Respect is an important part of Karate and what is learned can be put into practice in everyday life. Sensei Yogi's definition describes both Uechi Ryu and Pangai Nun as contradictory in their aspects of "hard" and "soft," and in that sense they are similar to Goju Ryu. Focus on the center of balance is an important characteristic of Uechi Ryu. The techniques emanate from the center of the body; movements are executed close to the body.

Tetsuhiro Hokama, who acted as interpreter during the interviews, is himself a renowned Grand Master of Karate and an accredited Historian on Okinawa. During our visit, Japanese Television was busy filming in his Dojo and Karate Museum and he was interviewed by a Japanese Karate magazine.

At the same time, Hokama was host to a delegation of high ranking Karate Grand Masters of the JKA in Japan, under the leadership of Shihan Seiichi Ohama from the Osaka Kyogashi Branch. Above all, the delegation was extremely interested in his Dojo and his unique Karate Museum.

Group of Grand Masters of the JKA who were visiting Tetsuhiro Hokama's Dojo

Comments made by Tetsuhiro Hokama Dr., PhD. in Karate, Dr.h.c., 10th Dan Karate Hanshi, 10th Dan Kobudo Hanshi, 10th Dan Kyusho Jutsu Hanshi, President of the Okinawan and International Goju-Ryu Kenshi-Kai Karate Do, Kobu-Do Association, (62 years old):

Tetsuhiro Hokama with Sansetu Kon

Tetsuhiro Hokama defines Okinawan Karate as a combination of weaponless techniques (Karate, Tuite and Kyusho Jutsu) and techniques using weapons (Kobudo). In his opinion one may only speak of a true Okinawan Master when he has complete command of both, the entire spectrum. With mastery in only one discipline, one is referred to as a teacher.

Traditional Training Methods in Hokama's Dojo in Nishihara

7 Cultural Differences in How the Human Body is Viewed

While the western world places more emphasis on an analytical view of the human body, many Asian countries have seen it, in the past, from an holistic and functional point of view. Western medicine divides the human body into anatomically oriented entities. As a result, the description of an illness relates primarily to individual organs and the human body is often regarded in the same way.

Functions related to single components such as tendons, muscles and bones are investigated and analyzed separately. Traditional Chinese medicine has a completely different approach in that it places emphasis on functional systems. This means that disturbances (illness) can be interpreted as an imbalance of energies. The Chinese conceive the universe as belonging to a higher principle described as Tao. In Tao we find the elements of Yin and Yang.

Everything in this universe which is connected with the feminine, moon, darkness and earth is assigned to Yin. All masculine things, such as sun, light and heaven are assigned to Yang.

In China, a body bowed to work in the fields, illustrates an example of a description of bodily sections in terms of Yin and Yang. Yin refers to those parts which remain in shadow when working in the rice fields, and Yang describes those parts which are exposed to the sun. The western world talks of inside and outside, missing the relationship to the sun and to the various parts of the body hidden in shadow. Yet it is exactly this differentiation which is essential to the Martial Arts, as will be explained later. This difference in orientation is the cause of numerous communication problems between the different cultures, not only with regard to medicine but also with respect to the Martial Arts.

The meridian system of Asian medicine, in particular, was absorbed into systems of combat in order to precisely locate the sensitive points of the body. Where western medicine sees attacks on certain points as having a mechanical effect, Chinese medicine views these as interruptions to the flow of energy (Qi) leading to a temporary, delayed or permanent disruption of function. The empirically obtained knowledge about the functions of the meridian system is so complex and detailed that it is practically impossible to note them all. The written version of the "Bubishi," the Bible of Okinawan Karate, extracted 12-36 from over 360 vital acupuncture points for use when attacking the human body. These are the most effective points which have crystallized out of centuries of experience for their particular effect on the human body.

This knowledge is valuable as it can be applied without much exertion in combat, which implicitly gives a significant tactical advantage, also without causing severe physical injury or damage to the opponent. There are seven forbidden zones in the Bubishi which have been identified to avoid serious harm. We assume that the Bubishi documents are a condensed version of the original knowledge about sensitive body points. A number of working groups were able to demonstrate additional points with good effectiveness, which are not quoted in the Bubishi. We should mention that not all acupuncture points are suitable for combat. It would be impossible to incorporate the multitude of effective points when making tactical decisions in combat.

The Bubishi's concentration on 36 effective points is the necessary consequence of having to find a pragmatic, simple solution. The following chapters contain not only theoretical details, but also details on their implementation in the use (Bunkai) of the Kata. Again, as evidenced by "Bubishi," there is a close relationship between the history of the traditional Kata and the development of Karate. The prospect of utilizing not only mechanical techniques in combat (twisting and over-stretching of joints, separating tendons and muscles from bone) but also being able to cause functional disruption to the meridian system of the opponent, presents a much larger spectrum for tactical action.

The probability of winning, despite physical inferiority, is dramatically improved.

8 The Importance of Acupuncture in Karate

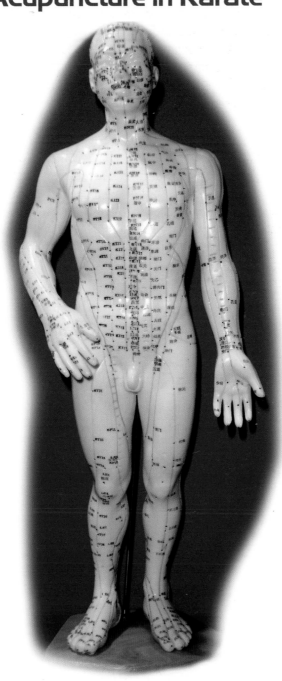

A significant part of Karate Kata is made up of exercises from Jintai Kyusho. These techniques were originally developed in China in line with the acupuncture system of traditional Chinese medicine. We cannot therefore understand the Kyusho techniques without having a basic knowledge of the anatomy of acupuncture. The following is a condensed presentation of the principle of the meridians. In order to explain this complicated medical system, it is necessary to simplify it to make it easier for the layperson to understand. Those wishing to delve deeper into the subject should make use of the available literature on acupuncture, acupuncture atlases and neurophysiology.

One can imagine the human body as a system of circuits similar to the electrical network of a large building. The building's network consists of cables allowing electricity to flow, which we can compare to the flow of energy, Qi. Its control sensors are equivalent to the sensors for our circulatory system, blood oxygen and so on. The resistors which prevent an explosive energy flow equate to the nerve centers in our spinal cord or the network of nerves in our abdominal cavity. Its capacitors for storing energy are the extra meridians, regulators, which function as compensators in the case of disruption or disturbance. In other words, it is a huge network of cables for connecting different functional units, the whole of which is monitored by another network of computers just as our body is monitored by its brain. Up to a certain point it can regulate itself. Larger disturbances, however, will cause partial failure or, in the worst case, a complete breakdown of the regulating system, as can also occur with the body.

Of course, the human nervous system is much more complex and research is on-going. The large network of cables used in acupuncture is like that of the autonomous nervous system. This system of nerves cannot be deliberately influenced. It provides fundamental impulses for the regulation of the heart, circulatory system, inner organs, pain, reflexes and much more.

The surface of the body, the skin, has small depressions varying between 1 and 5 millimeters in size, which house fine branches of nerves with direct contact to the meridians (energy paths) of the body. These depressions are acupuncture points. They are, so to speak, sensors over which energy can be fed in or drawn out. As mentioned above, this sort of impulse probably takes place over the fibers of the autonomous nerve system. In Kyusho these sensors and nerves are agitated solely at a fixed angle and direction. They possibly function in the same way as piezoelectric elements (the crystals in a cigarette lighter which provide the spark to light the flame).

The autonomous nerve system is an old and essential structure of nerves and comprises two seemingly contradictory components: the parasympathetic and the sympathetic nervous system. The sympathetic nervous system can be assigned to Yang, and the parasympathetic to Yin. This makes it easier to comprehend the Asian view of the body. The small nerve fibers of the autonomous nervous system run with blood vessels, lymph vessels and the nerve bundles. They also run through connective tissue of muscles and tendons as well as through the organs.

In layman's terms, acupuncture makes it possible to use the many funnel-shaped points on the outer surface of the skin to make contact with the deeper energy paths, the inner organs and the central nervous system (brain, spinal cord). It is rather like using a telephone to make contact with the inner organs and the nervous system. This contact with sensitive nerve points on the outer surface of the body can cause different nerves to be so agitated that this evokes given reactions in the opponent, independent of the anatomical region, the strength of the energy flow and independent of time. The "Bubishi", Okinawa's secret document, reduces the usual 360 acupuncture points to 12 – 36 vital sensitive points. It is indeed plausible that the system was deliberately simplified and limited to the most effective points. Once again, the Bubishi quotes seven forbidden zones which are so dangerous they should be avoided. In Okinawa's Martial Arts, Dim-Mac (identical to Kyusho) differentiates between five intensities in Jintai Kyusho:

1. Hun Xue: points which cause loss of consciousness

2. Ya Xue: regions which cause numbness, with inability to react

3. Ma Xue: points which lead to paralysis

4. Si Xue: points which are lethal

5. Mu Xue: regions which result in multiple complications, mostly in combination (They are attributed with a possible delayed death.)

Respective explanations according to western medicine:

1. Neurological disruption with loss of consciousness.

2. Nerve damage with usually temporary numbness in certain body areas.

3. Nerve damage with usually temporary paralysis to the arm or leg.

4. Injury to an anatomically delicate region (e.g. temples, brain, neck, heart region).

5. Injury with malfunctions, with partially delayed effect (e.g. rupture of the liver, damage to the veins in the legs, kidney and/or spleen, tear in bladder, thrombosis with delayed lung embolism and others).

There are 12 different primary meridians which are connected "inwards" with 11 inner organs, and " outwards" with the limbs and joints, as they were referred to in old China. There are also 8 extra (or wonder) meridians which build a network of connecting paths between the single meridians, 12 diverging channels (openings), 12 muscle channels and 12 skin regions. According to Asian teachings, power (Qi) and blood (Xue) flow through the 12 primary meridians, and spread through the connecting channels and diverging channels into the entire body over muscle- and skin channels. There are numerous accessible points (channels) on the surface of the meridians which can be used in acupuncture for medical treatment. There are over 360 well-known points of acupuncture as well as descriptions of extra and new points. An excess of energy (Qi) is re-routed to the extra meridians and stored there. When required, this stored energy (Qi) is then successively fed back into the primary meridians.

The Yang meridians lie on the outer (posterior) side of the arms and legs. The Yin meridians are located on the inner (anterior) side. Energy always flows in each meridian (energy transfer) in the same fixed direction. All of the meridians are connected by diverging and converging paths. The flow of Qi takes place in a rhythm of 24 hours, with fixed regularity, and is described as a daily cycle. There is a twice-daily flow for all meridians. Blood and Qi are flooded throughout the pathways at 2-hour intervals (see simplified organic clock) and achieve their maximum within this period of time. The flow of power over the 8 extra meridians happens on a permanent basis, independent of time. The so-called circadian rhythm and the phases of the sun and moon can be traced back to the Chinese Feng Yiyuan and to the Tao monk Liu Yuan.

The particular features of the circadian rhythm are utilized both in traditional Chinese medicine and in Asian Martial Arts. Massage techniques which follow the pathway of the flow of Qi are considered to be more effective than techniques which go in the opposite direction. An acupuncture point on the meridian which is struck by a blow during the phase of its highest flow of power is more seriously affected by this interruption to its Qi flow. Stimulation of these points 2-4 hours after the maximum flow of power can have a sedative effect in acupuncture when correctly used. The "Bubishi" describes numerous combinations of blows and kicks which make use of the circadian rhythm. The Chinese tradition of using signs of the zodiac to define a period of time was carried over into the Bubishi description for time periods, called Shichen. If we compare the times recorded in the Bubishi documents with those for maximum activity in the meridians according to the principles of acupuncture, we find there are quite a few discrepancies which cannot be explained. Unfortunately, it is still not clear whether this may have been a mistake in translation or in documenting the Bubishi.

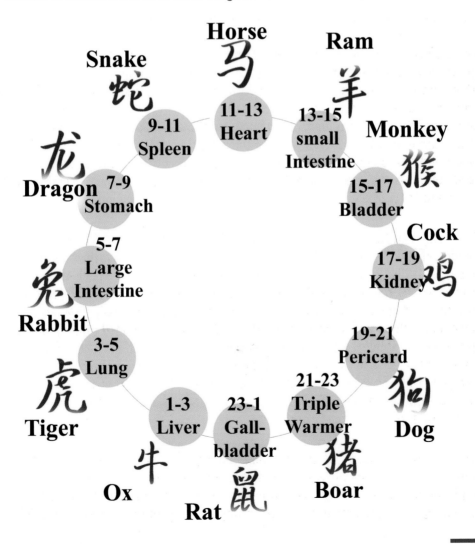

Simplified Organic Clock

The circadian cycle of energy flow (Qi) and blood flow (Xue) begins in the lungs (3-5 a.m.) and moves in a given path through the various meridians. The cycle ends in the liver. In TCM (traditional Chinese medicine) there are many cycles which are dependent on the time of day, which must be taken into consideration when treating illnesses. The phases of the moon also have a certain influence, as do the seasons and points of the compass.

The circadian rhythms are also partially known in western medicine. All of us have experienced the strong effect that our day-and-night rhythm can have on our organic functions. It governs our hormone production, our circulatory system, our digestive system, just to mention a few. However, this has not yet been thoroughly researched and there is a lack of remove solid material on the underlying phenomena. TCM can offer the West more information, by virtue of its different orientation and perspective and the volume of information accrued over the generations. Hokama tells us that Chinese time differentiation was much more complicated than shown here. Day and night were not only divided into 12 units of 2 hours each. Each time unit was named after an animal and was again divided into 4 sub-units for precision (e.g. Ox three = three-thirty). There is another time system parallel to this: morning and afternoon have six units, and midday and midnight have the number 9. These time units have numbers, not animal names. The calculation of time is therefore different. The circadian rhythm is altered by the seasons of the year and is governed by sunrise and sunset. The time-scheme is complemented by a compass with 12 points. Each point has a fixed zodiac name. The system is extremely complicated. At the higher levels of the Martial Arts, particular combinations for attack are recommended for particular times of day and with a defined compass direction. As the Chinese were well-schooled in this type of thinking, it was easy for them to work with this system for time and acupuncture. Knowledge of the circadian rhythm was allegedly used in the 36 chambers of the Shaolin to optimize the effect of training. The Kata were practiced at a given time of day and facing given points of the compass. The number "36", here, is purely symbolic and was used in old China to mean "numerous."

Meridians

Yin Meridians (inner) blue, Yang Meridians (outer) red

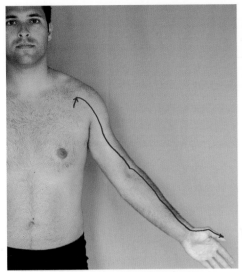

Lung meridian, Lu (11 Points) inside

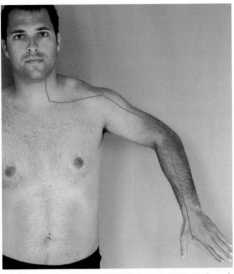

Large Intestine meridian, LI (20 Points) outside

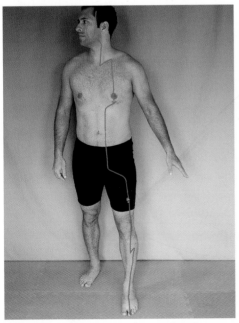

Stomach meridian, St (45 Points) outside

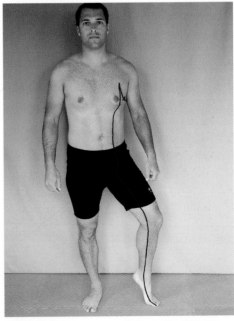

Spleen-Pancreas-meridian, Sp (21 P) inside

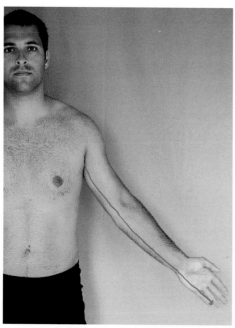

Heart meridian, He (9 Points) inside

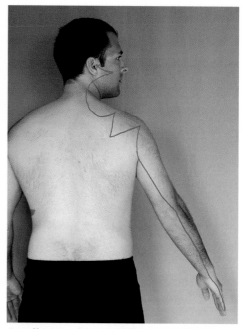

Small Intestine meridian, SI (19 Points) outside

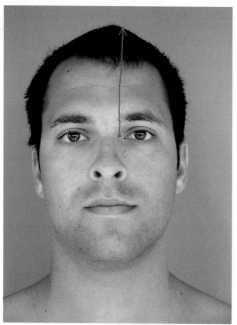

Bladder meridian, Bl (67 Points)

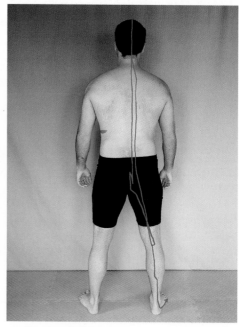

on the backside

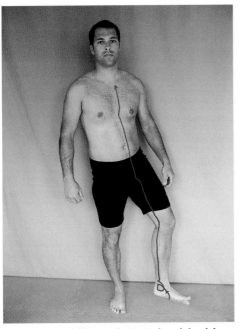

Kidney meridian, Ni 27 Points) inside

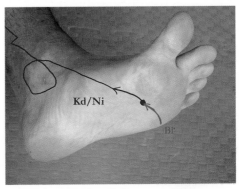

Cross to Bladder-Kidney meridian

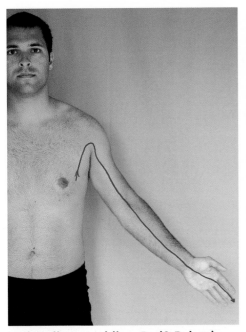

Pericardium meridian, Pe (9 Points) inside

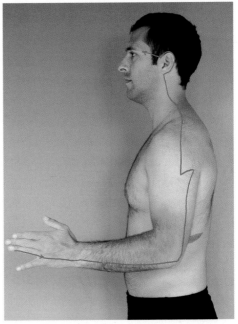

Triple Warmer, TW (23 Points) outside

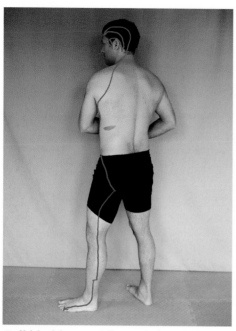

Gall bladder meridian, Gb (44 Points) outside

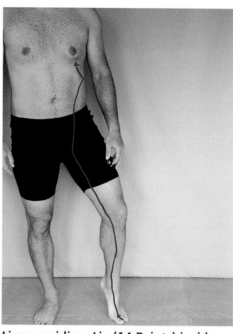

Liver meridian, Liv (14 Points) inside

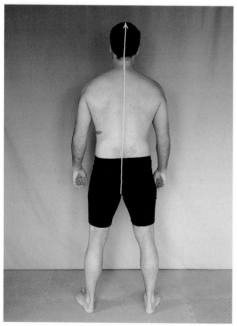

Governing Vessel, GV, Du Mai (28 Points)outside

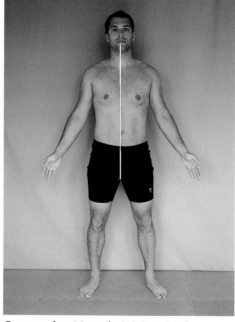

Conception Vessel, CV, Ren Mai (24 Points) inside

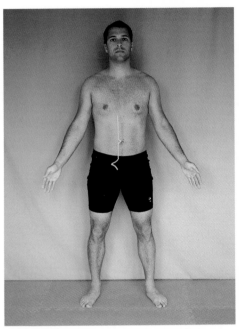

Penetrating Meridian, Chong Mai
(12 Points)

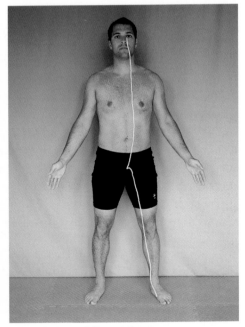

Girdling Meridian, Dai Mai (4 Points)

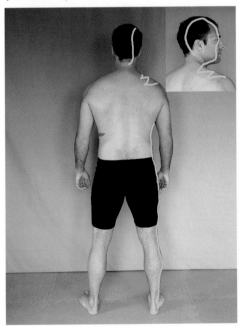

Yang Heel Meridian, Yangqiao
(13 Points)

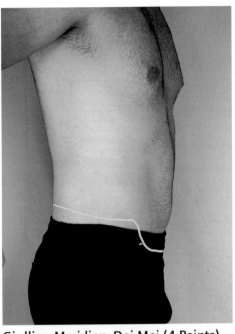

Yin Heel Meridian, Yinqiao
(5 Points)

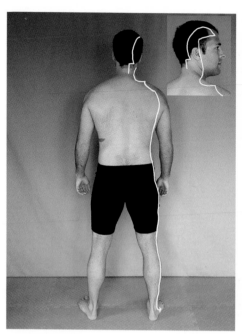
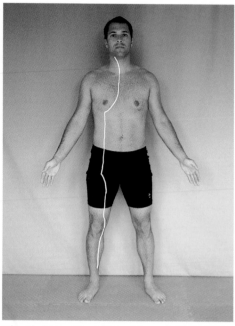

Yang Linking Meridian, Yangwei (15 Points)

Yin Linking Meridian, Yinwei (7 Points)

The Relationship between Kyusho and Healing

The Art of Kyusho Jutsu, which had been passed down through generations, continued to live in Grand Masters such as Soken Hohan (1891–1982), George A. Dillman's teacher, and a few other Masters. It was often so that these Masters had some medical education and it was, therefore, easier for them to obtain knowledge of the sensitive nerve pressure points of the body (Kyusho points). However, they were not primarily concerned with teaching their advanced, trusted students how to use potentially lethal techniques. The central focus of Kyusho Jutsu is to strike an attacker in a way which discourages him from continuing on, or places him in a situation where he no longer has full control of his body. It should result in as little serious or permanent damage as possible.

The "Bubishi" combinations were, in part, misinterpreted; it was alleged that death would follow after a given time. Hokama explained that this is typical of mistakes which arose in translating the old Chinese characters. In fact, the original Bubishi texts talk about neutral functional disruptions to the body. According to the teachings of TCM these can also be restored. Other critical points of attack are defined by the Bubishi as forbidden, as underlined by the mainly reserved and defensive focus of Okinawa's Martial Arts. If we analyze the Kata of various traditional styles more exactly, we can readily recognize a lot of Kyusho techniques. It is astounding to see just how large the repertoire of one single Kata can be. Gichin Funakoshi's statement that "every defense is an assault" and vice versa is true in more ways than one. A maximum of sensitive nerve points are subject to attack during assault and during defense alike.

9　The Role of　Bubishi

There are two versions of the so-called "Bubishi" which emerge from the Chinese province of Fukien. The first version was probably recorded in 1621 during the Ming Dynasty by Mao Yuan Yi, a war expert. This work consists of 240 chapters dealing mainly with the tactical side of warfare, for example in various terrains. It has similarities to what was written down by Sunzi. The book also deals with defending oneself against a weapon and combat techniques without the use of weapons. It describes 32 combat positions for weaponless defense, 16 of these with a partner. The original is kept under lock and key and is only supposed to be accessed by persons of high military ranking (R. Habersetzer).

The second version is said to have come from the Chinese village of Yong Chun in Fukien. It contains more combinations for use in combat, though no chapters on tactical warfare. The old language used is very difficult for a Chinese to understand, some is incomprehensible. It consists of 32 chapters. One chapter deals with the White Crane Style (Hakutsuru-Ken) or the Playing Crane, the points of acupuncture with regard to combat techniques and herbal treatment of illnesses and injuries. This chapter is difficult not only in terms of the language but also in terms of the content itself. Herbal recipes in China vary from region to region and the plants used in different areas of China vary in the concentration of their substances and composition.

The Chinese word "Bubishi" is derived from Bu "warrior", Bi "knowledge" and Shi "mind". Documentation goes as far back as Shaolin Kenpo, in which 365 so-called points of injury are given. There are descriptions of 36 blows and 24 paralyzing techniques (large points). In addition, there are descriptions of seven forbidden zones to which a blow can lead to irreversible damage. The documents of the second "Bubishi" were copied by hand and passed down from Master to Master. Again, inconsistencies in the documents are attributed to mistakes made in interpreting the old Chinese symbols, and also because each Martial Arts expert automatically brings with him his own experiences and perspective. Several Okinawan Masters have such copies, or have translated and analyzed various old Chinese copies, as Tetsuhiro Hokama has done.

Apparently examples can be found on the Japanese mainland which deal with the Jintai (Kyusho) version of the "Bubishi" (R. Habersetzer). Goju Kensha Master, Tadahiko Ohtsuka, published a work on the "Bubishi" in 1934. It consists of three chapters: 1. The History of the Crane Style, the Playing Crane (Happoren), Crane Style Techniques in Bubishi, 2. Introduction to Martial Arts, with an Introduction by Sunzi, Escape Techniques (Gedatsuho) and The Six Hand Forms (Rokkishi), and

3. Herbal Treatment of Injuries. Robert Habersetzer wrote an excellent German-language commentary on the Bubishi in 2004. A similar version was produced in English in 1995 by Patrick McCarthy, who previously worked with T. Hokama on Okinawa on this subject.

Tetsuhiro Hokama himself released a book in Japanese on this theme in 1984 under the name of "Okinawan Karate no Ayumi.". The similarities in the documents are plain to see. The writings of both Chojun Miyagi and Funakoshi also contain elements and basic principles originating from the "Bubishi."

To be able to understand the particularities of the Bubishi, it is necessary to first have basic knowledge of the acupuncture techniques of traditional Chinese medicine (TCM), and, of course, adequate knowledge of the human anatomy.

Without this knowledge the "Bubishi" will remain a closed book. However, the fact that the original documents were written using old Chinese symbols (some of which date back over 500-700 years) hampers our ability to decipher their full meaning.

Hokama's Research on Bubishi

Tetsuhiro Hokama spent decades on his studies of the "Bubishi" and the result of this analysis is his book "Okinawa Karate no Ayumi," extracts from which he made available to me for translation. It completely surpasses any other publications I would be able to obtain on this subject.

The "Bubishi" documents concern themselves with various areas:

1. Instructions for training

2. Tactical advice for combatants (similar to the book by Sunzi)

3. Typical combinations for self-defense (47 picture plates)

4. Happoren techniques (Crane Style)

5. A selection of Kyusho combinations (attacking sensitive neural reflex points)

6. The seven forbidden Kyusho zones

7. Diagnosis for wounds and injuries

8. Excerpts on herbal medicine for combatants

9. Fundamental knowledge of Kappo (techniques of revival)

10. The Tower Principle of the Five Circles and the Kyushos of the human body

11. The six Hand Forms (typical Hand Forms of Okinawa Te)

Hokama's interpretations are made with an awareness of the cultural uniqueness of the Asian mentality which gives us deeper insight into the background of the Martial Arts.

My time spent studying under Sensei Hokama taught me the value of learning at the source. When analyzing a situation of self-defense he always goes back to combinations out of the Goju Ryu Kata and compares these with the basic principles described in the combinations of the "Bubishi". Connecting the movements of the Kata with the rules of the Bubishi is a significant aid for orientation in the application (Bunkai) of Karate. He also clearly differentiates between the Omote, all "obvious" techniques, and the Okuden, the "hidden" techniques. His new book on the Bunkai of the Goju Ryu Kata interprets a substantial number of useful applications.

In no way do I see this as regressing to apparently out-dated Karate techniques. On the contrary, this is an excellent way of checking the effectiveness of modern combinations.

Combination to escape a grapple from behind, according to picture plate 27 from the "Bubishi," similar to a movement from the Seienchin Kata.

These very old techniques (Karate, Quanfa and Chinese Kempo), which matured over thousands of years, found their way into the "Bubishi" and have now become templates for developing new combinations in the hands of Okinawan Grand

Masters of today, such as Tetsuhiro Hokama. Over generations these Grand Masters have used their knowledge of the components of the combative arts and its practice to hone it to such perfection that they actually live their Art. This is a fundamental part of the culture of the people of Okinawa: similar to the Bushido of selected mainland Japanese and the Martial Arts of the Samurai, they continue to preserve a unique flower of their culture. In addition, unbelievable efforts have been made on the mainland with regard to the systematization of Judo, Karate and other Martial Arts and spreading them throughout the world.

In the hands of the Grand Masters of Okinawa and mainland Japan, the Martial Arts have a dimension which largely remains unseen by the average western world. Much remains a mystery because of our western perspective, mentality and approach to problem-solving. We can only achieve deeper insight into their culture with more intense involvement. I believe it is only possible to achieve real understanding of Karate, Judo, Aikido and other disciplines when one has sufficiently grasped the principles of traditional Chinese medicine. This does not stop with the study of the meridian system and acupuncture, but extends to the essential Asian concept of health, of the desire to live with and within nature, and on to the breathing forms of Tai Chi and Qi Gong.

The Historical Development of Kyusho Jutsu

It is difficult to trace back the historical development of Kyusho Jutsu and Tuite Jutsu in the Asian Martial Arts as their early experts and Masters originally made no written records (around 1300). This was also sometimes the case in later times. Furthermore, the tradition was to pass down secret techniques to chosen members of the family or to very trusted advanced students under certain circumstances. Kyusho Jutsu is closely related to the acupuncture model of traditional Chinese medicine.

Zhan San-Feng was possibly the first to develop a system of vital points on a large scale in China around 1300, called Dim-Mac (Erle Montaigue). It is said that Zhang, a hermit living in the Wudang Mountains, tested typical acupuncture points on animals and then later on humans by using strike and pressure techniques to check the result. Zhang, who lived in the Hopei Province, was so impressed by the effectiveness of these techniques that he stopped writing them down. Instead he passed his knowledge directly on to members of the family and hid the various techniques in the form of dance movements, the so called **h'ao ch'uan**, which later became Taiji Quan.

The first form of documentation was probably undertaken by his student, T'sung-yeuh (Erle Montaigue, R. Habersetzer). This knowledge is likely to have found its way to Buddhist monasteries which were intensively interested in herbal medicine and the combative arts. One example is the technique of the Poisoned Hand, the Dianxue (Xue = cavity, blood flow).The name Poisoned Hand reflects the partially delayed effect which occurred hours or days later and is generally connected with the circadian rhythm and the flow of power through the meridians. There was a gradual development of varying styles such as Shaolin Kenpo (classified as a very hard form which gave the impulse for later development of Shorin Ryu on Okinawa), as well as the Yang system, with softer movements which possibly had an influence on the Goju Ryu of Okinawa.

With their proximity to Taiwan and China, the Ryu Kyu islands (and Okinawa, in particular) were, predestined for cultural exchange between China and Japan. This obviously applied to the Martial Arts for self-defense as well. Even when traveling to Okinawa today, it is still easy to see the cultural influence of the Chinese, Japanese, Philippines and others in the architecture, gardens, living design and above all, in the population itself . Okinawa originally had a specific form of self-defense known as Ti (also pronounced Te). Around 1400, this system was influenced by elements of Shorinji Kenpo (Chinese: Kenpo). Once again, it was handed down by word-of-mouth and not in writing. It was also strongly influenced by Zen-Buddhism which was brought to China around 520 A.D. by the Indian monk, Dharuma (known as Bodhidharma in India). He was renowned for meditation (Za Zen) in which he supposedly spent a period of nine years. His teachings on physical and mental training were called Ekkinkyu. Two books were discovered in the Shorin Temple (Shaolin Temple), which were referred to as Ekkinkyu and Senzuikyo (T. Hokama). The contents of Ekkinkyu were passed down by various Masters to the inhabitants to Okinawa as Shorinji Kenpo, or Chinese Kenpo. The Ekkinkyu was incorporated into Okinawa's system of self-defense, which then gave rise to Okinawan Te (T. Hokama).

There are doubts about the connection between Buddhism and the later-to-emerge Karate. Master Arakaki, for example, believes that two styles, Shorin Ryu and Shorei Ryu, were brought to Okinawa from China and that both influenced later styles of Karate (T. Hokama). The Martial Arts have always been closely connected with the art of herbal medicine, whether in India, China, Korea, Okinawa, and later Japan. This led to the emergence of healing methods and revival techniques such as Kappo, Kuatsu, Jin Shin Jyutsu, among others. They were also important for the prevention of injury. Unfortunately it seems that knowledge of the traditional healing methods is slowly disappearing and is partially being replaced by modern western medicine, even in Japan. In our eyes this is a most regrettable trend, not that the different methods of western and Asian medicine should be treated as competing methods, for they are complementary, one to the other. However, Western school medicine concentrates on the treatment of organ damage, and traditional Chinese medicine places its emphasis on treating regulatory disturbance to various organ systems. There is also more of an orientation stressing prevention of harm and illness than in western medicine. Okinawa was repeatedly overrun by foreign conquerors and the use of weapons had been forbidden more than once (in 1470 and 1609). Combat techniques incorporating attacks on vital points were secretly trained on Okinawa and were disguised as "folk dances," the Odoris. There was a situation similar in China and Korea.

Essential information on the Martial Arts is found in the "Bubishi" (of which only a few copies exist), which were copied by hand from the original Chinese texts. Funakoshi quotes important material from the old Chinese Masters, the "Bubishi" in his books. One of the first to further develop Okinawan Te was Sakugawa Kanga (born 1733). Matsumura Sokon (born ca. 1798) studied the combative arts under Sakugawa and under the Chinese Master, Kong Shu Kung, who created the Karate Kata Kushanku (later Kanku Dai). Among Matsumura's students were: Itosu Anko, Kuwate Ryusei, Yabu Kensetsu, Hanashiro Chomo, Kyan Chotoku and Gichin Funakoshi.

Very interesting studies can be made over the step-by-step concealment of Kyusho Jutsu techniques by reading and analyzing Gichin Funakoshi's books chronologically.

Erwin Baelz, M.D., a German medical doctor and college professor who was working under a teaching contract at the Imperial University in Tokyo, motivated Jigoro Kano to transform the Jujutsu system into something which would be more suitable for the physical education of young Japanese, similar to what Jahn (the "father of gymnastics") had done in Germany. Jigoro Kano encouraged Funakoshi to create something for Karate which would be similar to that which Kano did for Judo. The Martial Arts needed to be lifted up above the level of pure self-defense and military combat. He was looking to create a system suitable for physical education, character improvement, and for competitive sport while, at the same time, reducing the risk of injury. The result was an incredible intellectual achievement by Masters Kano and Funakoshi, in the areas of Judo and Karate – both of which originated from the Jutsu system. Both systems were made decisively less dangerous. The traditional Karate Kata were modified and realistic implementation defused.

Training schemes were altered and the secret, somewhat dangerous, techniques were not passed on to students.

It is only in the traditional Kata that the real Kyusho techniques can be recognized in their use (Bunkai) through reconstruction, comparison with older versions and other interpretations. Kyusho techniques (techniques for a strike to vital points) and Tuite techniques (pressure points for twisting of joints) are encoded in Kata. One of Gichin Funakoshi's first books, entitled "To Te Jutsu" includes an older form of Kanku Dai (Kushanku) which was taken to Okinawa in 1761 by the Chinese Kenpo Master, a special Delegate sent by the Ming Emperor Kong Shu Kung (Japanese: Kosokun). This was the origin of Kanku Sho and Kanku Dai in Shotokan Karate. This Kata is trained in Shorin Ryu as Kusanku and is probably the older version as it contains more authentic elements than Shotokan. Earlier books written by Funakoshi (with partners) also show combinations in which the withdrawn fist does not rest stylistically on the hip but, true to its purpose, draws back the opponent's hand as a method of gathering more power into the attacking fist and at the same time upsetting the opponent's balance (G.A.Dillman).

Funakoshi's later books show these authentic techniques in a more stylized manner which conceals them from the eyes of the person in training. True to the tradition of Japanese Bujutsu "the war skills of the Samurai", lessons were divided into: Shoden, "basic" techniques, chuden "advanced" techniques, and okuden "secret" techniques. These days most of the techniques of Kyusho Jutsu remain hidden even from most Karate Masters because there are so few qualified to teach them who have researched these techniques or have received instruction from Japanese Masters. Menkyo Kaiden (Master Qualification) is a level which is only accessible to special, chosen Masters. It is simply not possible to understand Kyusho Kutsu without having an adequate level of anatomical knowledge and knowledge of the rules of acupuncture.

As a result it is only too easy to dismiss the techniques as charlatanism or pass them on incorrectly. The real character of Ryu Kyu Kenpo is bedded in Kyusho Jutsu, and this can be most impressively demonstrated by a row of Okinawan Masters such as Tetsuhiro Hokama and also several western working groups.

B Special Part

I Coded Kata Techniques in Karate – Cracking the Code

1.1   Ready Position (Yoi)

When starting to learn Karate, assuming the Ready Position would seem to have no particular significance other than that of etiquette and assuming a fighting position (Sanchin). The actual combat-related tactical background is complex, however, and entails more than readiness for possible conflict. The initial movement of every Karate Kata displays elements of self-defense and resistance as well as elementary movements and performances arising from Qigong. It is extremely difficult to discover and appreciate the real meaning of these movements without knowledge of the cultural background of their Chinese origin. In the following we will take a step-by-step look at various details.

When assuming the Ready Position (Yoi) one foot (usually the left foot) is placed at an outward angle, as in Qigong. The tilted pelvis means that two thirds of the body weight is borne by the front part of the foot, one third is carried by the heel. The basic position is in line with the theory of the Chinese meridians. The earth-energy should enter the body over the acupuncture point Kidney 1 on the sole of the front of the foot. Contact to the heavens is directed over acupuncture point Governing Vessel 20. According to the Chinese view, collected energy can exit the body over the points Pericardium 8 (Circuit 8), the palms of the hands.

Chinese Medicine sees the human body as a sort of lightning conductor between earth and the heavens, connecting between the acupuncture points Kidney 1 and Governing Vessel 20. The release of energy over the palms of the hands (Pericardium 8) is probably used in some religions as a form of "healing hands." According to Traditional Chinese Medicine (TCM), this energy form (Qi) flows over the numerous meridians, muscle channels and other connecting routes into the depths of the body to reach the organ systems and ensure its correct functioning with a defined daily rhythm. (See "The Importance of Acupuncture in Karate.")

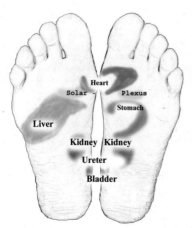

Ni 1, Chinese: Yongquan, Japanese: Yu Sen, English: Gushing Spring

Earth energy enters the body over Kidney 1 on the soles of the feet. The illustration shows the organs on the soles of the feet which are affected by foot reflex massage. The hands also have similar corresponding points for massage and acupuncture techniques. This fractal view (i.e. each small component complies with the overall

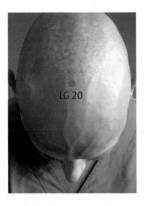

LG 20

Governing Vessel 20 is the connecting point for energy directed to the heavens LG 20, Chinese: Bai Hui, Japanese: Hyaku E, English: Hundred Convergences

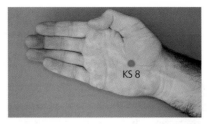

KS 8

Pericardium (Circuit 8) is the exit point for energy Ks8 = Pe8, Chinese: Lao Gong, Japanese: Ro Kyu, English: Palace of Toil

regulation of the entire body) is a basic principle of holism. In effect, training on bare feet and the use of one's bare hands activates a reflex massage for the entire body, assuming the exercises follow the rules.

In Karate the arms execute a small circular movement in front of the body with the fists closed, the hands move back to the hips and then downwards. The scale of movement in Qigong is larger though the movements are identical. In Qigong the arms are moved with open hands in a large circle over the head to be brought to rest in front of the body. In Karate the hands are mostly closed at the beginning of the Kata.

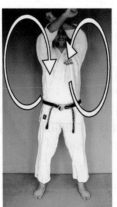

This larger movement brings one meaning to the fore. Several variations on defense techniques are possible as a starting movement. An opposing attack with a fist directed at the head can be deflected by an opening movement using a cross block (Jujii Uke) or a one-sided parry of the opponent's arm either inwards or outwards. The system of every Kata is designed so that a technique can be equally applied to both the right and the left. Interchanging the techniques – sometimes from the right, sometimes from the left – is relevant for both attacker and defender. In this way, every Kata presents a complete system of self-defense in itself, and develops both sides of the body during training and practice. In the Kata, the closed fists are moved towards the hips. In practice, the defending person grasps the attacker's wrist or sleeve and draws it back to the hips.

This generally disrupts the opponent's balance (Kuzushi), making it difficult for him to start a counterattack. This is a simple method of controlling the opponent and enabling one's own counterattack. These movements can also be used as a freeing technique and come out of the Chinese Chin Na system (grab and control). A look will be taken later at the different opening techniques for freeing oneself from various grips. The illustrations show merely some of the various possible applications. The movements of a Kata show patterns which can be compared to an outline of a sketch.

The possibilities for varying the movements and applications are many. It would not have been possible for a Kata to contain the complete combat system of a Master were the Bunkai not to allow for so much diversity in their interpretation. This means that the interpretation of a Kata can be individually developed from this basic pattern. The Kata presents a string of numerous techniques which do not have to be used in a specific sequence. A Kata also does not have to show combat against more than one opponent. The application is open in its variations and in its sequence.

The opening movement as a parry which simultaneously disrupts the attacker's balance.

Connection to Qigong

As already mentioned, the explanation of an opening movement goes further than the interpretation of its use in combat. It actually mirrors the Qigong philosophy. The description of the typical opening movement differs according to which School of Qigong we are looking at. The real intention of the opening movement in Qigong is to establish a connection between heaven, earth and the human. The Qi, in its original form, has to be renewed. It is important when carrying out this exercise that bodily awareness be intensified in relation to earth. The hips, abdomen and upper body should be relaxed. Imagining an extended line reaching from the buttocks to the earth should reinforce this feeling of being rooted within the earth. The tip of the tongue should rest lightly on the gums to close the meridians Governing Vessel (rear middle line) and Conception Vessel (front middle line). This technique supposedly hinders a knockout in Kyusho when a sensitive point is hit. Touching both arms connects the Yin (inner) and Yang (outer) meridians with one another. Resting the fists on the hips maintains contact with the Girdling Meridian which is the only meridian to connect all vertical meridians. The aim is to harmonize the Qi. The movements are coordinated with breathing techniques to achieve a conscious, deep and natural method of breathing. It should transfer concentration from the head to the abdominal region and function as a sort of massage for the inner organs. This increases awareness of gravity in the lower abdomen, namely the Tandien (CV6). The individual phases of the opening movement are named according to the respective School. Shi Xinggui Shaolin Qigong, for example, has the phases: connecting heaven and earth, breathe energy, open, connect, release and conclusion. In another School we find elements such as: "separate the clouds" or "rowing on a quiet sea", and other descriptions. The most essential thing is to understand that this simple movement in Karate is part of a larger context. Hidden behind the opening movement is the Chinese concept of preventative health gymnastics.

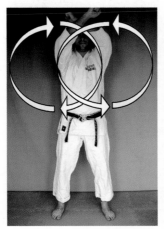 

The opening movement

1.2   Etiquette, The Bow (Re)

A full bow entails the open left hand meeting the closed right hand, whereby the open hand represents Yin and the closed hand is Yang. In the Martial Arts this movement goes beyond the actual greeting ritual to start an attack rising out of the defensive. The illustrations show that the head of the metacarpus on the right fist is able to hit several points and a strike to the head can result in a knock out. These points are: points Gb1 and TW (3E) 23 on the temple or, for example, Ex-HN-5 at the nerve exit points on the chin. This exemplifies the fact that every movement in Karate has more than one meaning. The open hand touches other points on the opposite side of the head.

Greeting Movement

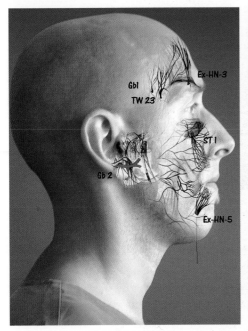

The Relationship of Acupuncture Points and Nerve Exit Points

Strike to Gb1 or TW23

Defense against Double Grip on Wrist

An opponent who has a grip with both hands on the wrist makes a counterattack difficult and freeing oneself with only one hand becomes almost impossible. With this in mind, the greeting movement now offers a further possibility for interpretation and application. This consists of freeing oneself with the aid of the second, open hand. Similar constellations can be found in the Kata Enpi, Bassai Dai and Seifa.

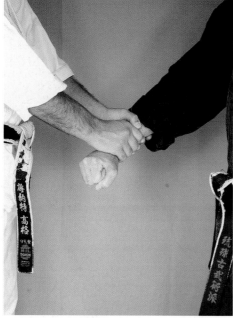
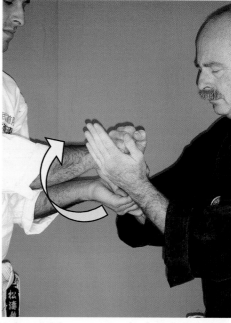

Gripping the wrist with both hands, freeing with open and closed hand by increasing leverage

Initial and Closing Defense

Even the closing phase of the finalizing movement of the complete Greeting shows a hidden attack arising out of the defense in the direction of CV6 (Tandien). Reinforcement of the spear hand (Nukite) by the underlying fist and an angle of attack of between 30 and 45° directed at the plexus of the pelvic organs allows for maximum effectiveness of the technique with a possible knock out even before the fight has begun. This application of what is, at first glance, a harmless greeting movement in the Kata is not immediately obvious. The effect of an attack on CV6 functions goes through the neuro-anatomical circuit in the plexus of the minor pelvis, over vegetative nerve fibers running segmentally to the spinal cord, and on further in the direction of the brain. The strike or stab causes an impulse there which results in a sudden drop in blood pressure and a subsequent loss of consciousness. Reinforcement of the spear hand (Nukite) by the underlying fist stabilizes the spear hand's outstretched finger.

Closing Movement in direction of CV6 (Nerve Center of the Pelvic Organs)

Segmental (tiered) connection of the nerves from the plexus to the spinal cord and front middle line (Conception Vessel). This activates a reflex curve which, although acknowledged by the brain, cannot be consciously influenced. A strike results in stimulation of the Nerve Center of the Pelvic Organs.

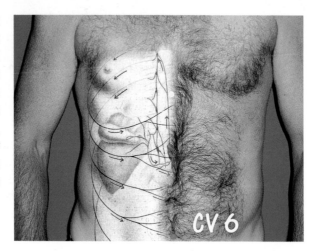

1.3 The Opening Movement (Iriguchi Waza)

1.3.1   In Jion, Jiin, Jitte

Each Kata begins with a different starting movement which, in turn, needs to be separately interpreted. Individual Kata groups may have similar starting movements. The following details the starting movements of the Kata Jion or Jiin and Jitte.

On the surface of things, it could be just a greeting. Additionally it could mean that no weapon is being used. Considering that we are probably taking a superficial view (Omote) we now need to ask what lies hidden below the surface. Keep in mind

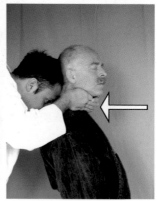

Firm grip of the hand   *Leverage on the wrist*   *Variation: throttling technique*

that the closed fist (Yang) rests in the open left hand (Yin) and that both hands are moved together towards the breast. The application arises out of this movement. If, for example, an attacker does not release the hand, we then have the chance of using both hands as shown below to apply leverage to the wrist. Another variation would be a throttling technique from behind, supported by counter pressure from the head.

The starting positions of the other Kata present numerous other possibilities of using leverage. Among these are Stretched Arm Leverage or Joint Leverage at the Wrist as shown below. This combination of the Yin and Yang position of the hands (one hand closed to form a fist, the other hand open) is often used in the Kata. This probably stems from the fact that the Karate Masters of old made the purely empirical discovery that the combination of Yin and Yang elements are often very effective when applying the Martial Arts. They also discovered that the combination of soft and hard techniques is more effective than using only hard movements or only soft techniques. Generally speaking, there is no sense in countering a hard attack with an equally hard block. In contrast, it is much more clever to divert the attacker's power or to avoid it.

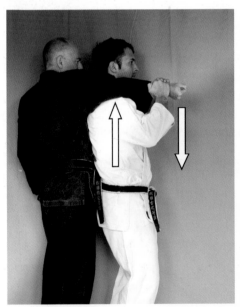 

Stretched arm lever, e.g. from Jion or Chinte   *Wrist lever from Jion, Jiin or Jitte*

The starting movement of the Chinte Kata presents a very effective technique arising out of a backward hop, which can lead to a broken elbow joint.

1.3.2   Starting Movement in Bassai Dai

In the Bassai Dai Kata one could once again assume that the hand position at the start of the Kata means simply that no weapon is present or will be used. Once again, the right fist rests in the left hand, i.e. the right fist is Yang, the open left hand is Yin. The first movement of the right fist is outwards (Yang) and the left hand moves inwards (Yin). The left palm can be interpreted as soft and the right hand, or fist, as hard. The combination of hard and soft (Go and Ju) has the effect of reinforcing the technique in various applications. The starting movement is open to various possible interpretations of the Bunkai, some of which are set out below.

Initial Movement in Bassai Dai

Cross-gripping of the wrist, for example, means that the technique can be effectively used as a lever (Kote Gatame). This technique can be observed using open hands in several other Kata such as, for example, in a later phase of the Bassai Dai Kata, in the Kanku Dai Kata and in Kanku Sho. As with the other Kata, the transition from a closed fist to an open hand is flowing. This gives rise to an abundance of application techniques. Changing the angle of the opponent's elbow, shoulder joint and wrist is critical to the success of the Kote Gatame. Shortening the distance by Kousa Dachi on the part of the defender allows an outward pivot of the

Cross-gripping of the wrist

Kote Gatame (hand rotation lever)

The same technique with a longer lever

attacker's shoulder joint, an elbow joint bend of up to 90° and a 30-45° bend or twist of the wrist. Moving the left hand (i.e. diverging from the actual Kata movement) enables usage of the Nikyu lever from Aikido. Cross-gripping by the attacker at elbow level also allows the starting movement of the Bassai Dai Kata to be applied as a modified hand-bend and -rotate lever. These techniques are not obvious at first glance (Okuden).

The obvious meaning of the technique (Omote) is often interpreted as either defense with the open left hand or with the lower right arm (Soto Ude Uke), or again as an attack with the back of the fist (Uraken). The targets for the Uraken Uchi can, however, vary according to how the wrist has been turned. With CV 24 (Conception Vessel) we are talking about a sensitive point which can easily result in a KO when correctly applied with an angle of 45° from above in the direction of the chin. This is a typical point which is taught in Jintai Kyusho. There are numerous other target points on the head, for example, on the chin below the corner of the mouth (Ex-HN-5), in front of the angle of the jaw Stomach 5 or the side of the temple Gb1 (Gall Bladder) and TW 21 (Triple Warmer). All of these points are very sensitive nerve points from Kyusho. As a result the person struck is either dazed or unconscious. These points are mentioned in part in the Bubishi documents.

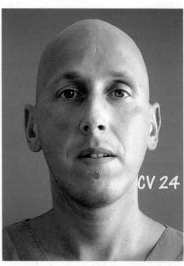

Uraken from the Kata Bassai Dai   *Strike to CV24 on the chin*

CV (Conception Vessel) 18 presents itself as a suitable target area of the body. It reacts in the same way as other acupuncture or Kyusho points in the Middle Line, above the breastbone, principally to friction. CV18 should preferably be hit with the small head of the fifth metacarpal bone, whereby once again the fist should come from above to meet the breastbone at an angle of 45°. The illustration shows how to hold the correct angle by the movement sequence of the Kata and the Kousa Dachi stance with rotation of the hips. A strike to the breastbone causes loss of breath. Similar movements can be found in modified form in other Kata such as, for example, the three Naihanchi Kata (Tekki).

  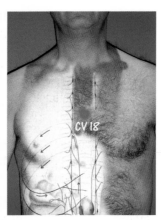

Various applications of Uraken from the Kata Bassai Dai

1.3.3   Starting Movement of the Kata Enpi

The Enpi Kata has a hand position in which the left hand is open and the right hand formed to a fist – again a representation of Yin and Yang. This hand position also occurs in the Seifa Kata in Goju-Ryu and enables various sudden wrist leverages which, when applied, cause injury to the attacker's wrist. The closed fist

Starting Movement of the Kata Enpi: Dropping to the knee and intensifying the downwards movement

can act as the gripping hand; the open hand is most likely to act as a lever reinforcement, i.e. to stop the attacker's hand. The sudden jerky hip movement can best be seen in the Seifa Kata. The movement is slower in the Enpi Kata in Shotokan. This may have been meant to camouflage the technique and may or may not have been introduced intentionally in the past. Exact details are not likely to come to the surface. The highest importance is placed on the fact that the technique can be individually used in different ways. The individual interpretation follows the ideas of several Okinawan Masters. The Kata requires only that the basic movement patterns be passed on. Primarily important is that the individual interpretation be functional in the application.

Various levers can be used in application of the first movement. For the variation shown here the elbow joint must be turned to the front by 45°. This means that the Gedan Barai can be used to strike either the stretching receptor (Golgi Apparat) of the triceps tendon immediately behind the processus of the Ulnar bone or the crossover point of the rear upper arm nerve (Nervus Radialis). This follows the principle that defense is not only defense but a counterattack, at the same time as Funakoshi has explained.

The Starting Movement from Enpi as Kote Gatame or as Elbow or Upper Arm Lever (Hit)

Both points refer once again to Kyusho points which have a direct connection to the abovementioned anatomical structures or nerves, these being the points Triple Warmer 11 (TW, SJ) or 12. A forceful strike from 45° forwards and upwards in the direction of the Nervus Radialis can lead to a KO. We can see that the Kata Enpi also offers a number of sensitive points of attack in the first sequence (Jintai Kyusho).

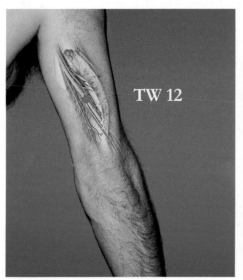
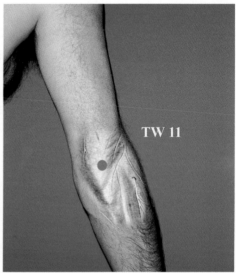

TW 12

TW 11

3E12 (TW 12) corresponds to the intersection of the weak Radial Nerve. 3E11 corresponds to the stretching receptor of the triceps tendon.

1.3.4   Starting Movement of Kanku Dai

The first movement of the Kata, in which the fingers of the hands form a triangle, has often given rise to speculation. In Qigong, this triangle represents the mouth of the tiger and is used in diverse meditative exercises. The Japanese interpret this hand position as a sign of the rising sun. Ninjutsu has several hand and finger positions which have different meanings. For the Ninjas, the triangular finger formation stands for the ring of the sun.

The finger sign Zai Nichi Rin is a reference to the five elements of space, earth, water, fire and wind which enables control over them. Getting past the symbolic character of this movement requires some thought. There are multiple applications of this starting movement in the Kanku Dai Kata. The Bunkai extends from freeing techniques to the simulation of throttling techniques and defending oneself against them. The closing movement also ends with the open hands being joined, whereby the left hand is on top and represents Yang, the hand beneath it representing Yin. This also has a deeper meaning in the application as explained below.

Opening Movement in Kanku Dai

When the wrists have been grabbed by an attacker it is easy to free oneself by moving your own hands inwards to break free. With the hand position as given in the Kata – using both hands – it is easier and more effective to free oneself in this way than by using your hands separately.

The triangular formation of the hands can be seen again in an attack with open throttling. Once again, the starting movement of the Kata offers a possible freeing action in the early phase of the strangle grip. Alternatively, one can start a counterattack by using a finger stab to the eyes.

Strangling   *Freeing movement*

Another interpretation of the movement gives the attacked person, when held by both wrists, the possibility of forming his hands into a fork and thereby releasing himself from the hold. This method of release is often used in Jujutsu or in Chin Na.

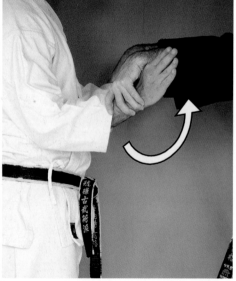

Gripping both hands and release by fork-like leverage

The closing movement of the first sequence can be so applied that the left hand strikes acupuncture point Bladder 59 to 61 and the right inner edge of the hand strikes Spleen point 6 (three Yin intersection, passageway for all Yin meridians) when the attacker uses a Mai Geri Chudan (straight kick to center body). The left hand hits Yang meridian points, the right hand strikes a Yin point. The attacker has a numb feeling in the lower leg, making him unsteady on his feet.

The second phase of the opening movement in Kanku Dai. Striking the point Spleen 6 (three Yin intersection) is most effective and causes numbness of the leg.

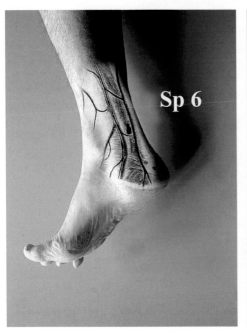

Sp 6

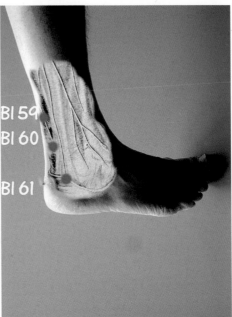

Bl 59
Bl 60
Bl 61

1.4　The Closing Movement (Degushi Waza)

The closing movement in every Kata can be used to hit an attacker. The following example illustrates a defender caught in a collar-hold. The arm is struck on the Kyusho (acupuncture) points Large Intestine 10 and 11. The most effective result is achieved by hitting with the small head of the metacarpus or with the edge of the hand. A hit to Large Intestine 11 or 10 results in the legs giving way

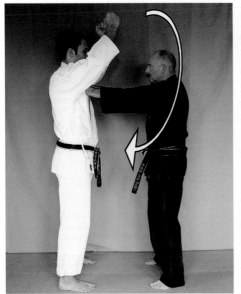

Hold on Collar

Hit to Li 10 or 11

and is often used in combination with additional attack moves in other Kata. The points Li 10 and 11 are co-related to a surface nerve on the forearm.

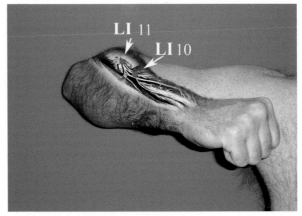

Anatomical reference to nerves

With the legs of the attacker bent, the defender can initiate his subsequent attack in the direction of CV 6 at an optimal downward angle of 45°. This technique was described in the closing bow ritual at the start of the chapter. Qi is drawn out of the body; a loss of consciousness can be caused by irritation to the pelvic nerve network.

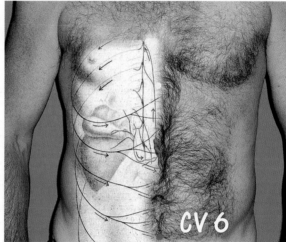

Stab to the lower abdominal plexus, Tiered structure of the nerves in the reflex curve

The closing movement complies with the sequence also practiced in Qigong. This allows for fulfillment of the formal, deeply-rooted cultural requirements.

1.5 Basic Techniques from Another Point of View

1.5.1   Withdrawal of the Fist to the Hips (Hikite)

The classic movement for a straight fist punch and other techniques is to withdraw the rear fist all the way to the hips. This is not merely a formality but a deliberate application. First, the elbow of the withdrawn hand can execute a defending hit to the rear and second, withdrawing and turning the rear hand is important for an escape action. It is relatively unimportant whether the attacker's hand grips the wrist on the same side or the crossed hand. In both cases the attacker is effectively brought out of balance, as shown, making it easier to counteract. With a same-sided grip, the drawback of the hand and turn upsets the attacker's balance and his upper body tilts slightly outward. The following illustrations show the sequence of movement in detail. An additional effect is that the force of the striking fist

Gripping the wrist, turning

Gripping the opponent's wrist withdrawing, disrupting balance

striking fist increases when the opponent is drawn into the technique. This principle can be utilized in both the forward stance (Zenkutsu Dachi) and when assuming the back stance (Kokutsu Dachi). The stance is used to influence the distance, i.e. increased disruption of the attacker's balance (Kuzushi).

Gripping the wrist with the opposite hand has the effect of swinging the opponent outwards and thus enables a downward elbow press or a counteraction with the other fist. Once again, this has the advantage of bringing the opponent fully under control. These actions usually function with the element of surprise. It is difficult to activate the relevant techniques when the opponent anticipates the counter. A lot of Kyusho techniques require the element of surprise to function as defense. This basically applies to all attacks because for each attack there is a counterattack.

1.5.2   Fist to Fist

Escaping, Controlling, Kyusho

Gripping the Wrist

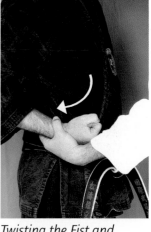

Twisting the Fist and pressing the metacarpus of the middle finger against Pericard 7

In the Kata one can often see one fist resting on the other fist on the hips. Again, this action has a deeper meaning not only with regard to an escape technique but also for the control and use of sensitive points (Kyusho). Turning the fist effectively weakens the opponent's hand, particularly when the small head of the metacarpus puts direct pressure on the point Pericard 7 (PC 7).

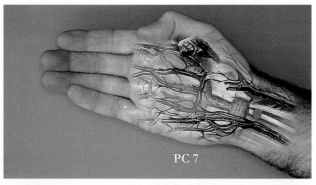

PC 7

PC 7 is located on the top of the middle Forearm Nerve (N. medianus)

Another application, often seen in Shito Ryu when executing the Kata, is using the knuckle of the middle finger (Ippon ken) to irritate the radius- or ulna-sided channel on the wrist by a downward rubbing movement. This stimulates the acupuncture points Lung 7-8 and Heart 5-6, hereby enormously weakening the opponent's wrist. One Ippon Ken hit to this region results in the grip being released immediately.

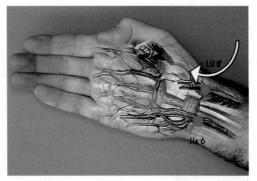

Gripping the wrist, rubbing the radial channel with Ippon Ken

Relationship of the acupuncture points Lung 8 and Heart 6 to the arm nerves and vessels

Another variation is a double-grip to the opponent's wrist and hand. This causes the upper body to be tilted outwards so that other countering techniques such as a punch or a throw (e.g. O Soto Gari, Large Outer Reap) can be activated.

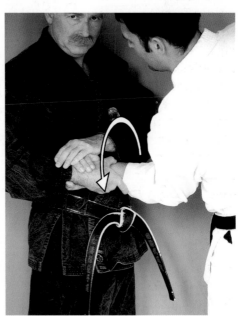

Angled wrist lock in double-grip

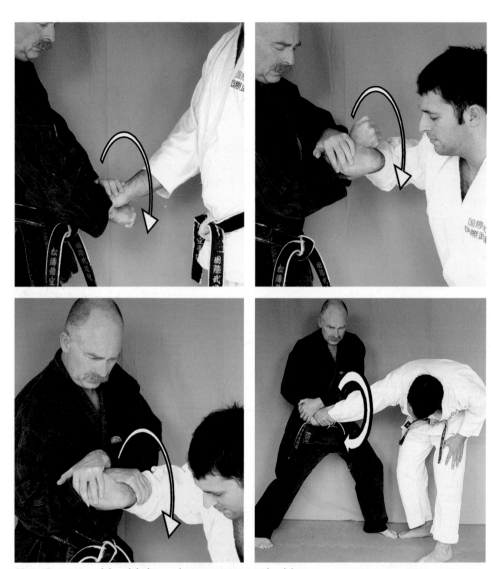

Kote Gatame with withdrawal movement to the hip

Depending on the type of hold, there are several variations for this sort of grip as the following illustrations show. The crossed-grip, in particular, allows the use of numerous other applications. Simply put, the Kata offers the opportunity to use a number of combinations and applications for realistic combat situations. These basic techniques are practiced over and over again in numerous Kata. They are the foundation of realistic self-defense, and can be found in other Martial Arts such as Japanese Jutsu, Aikido and modern Juijitsu.

1.5.3   Utilizing the Turning Movement

Turning movements in Shotokan are usually executed so that the rear leg is positioned in line with the opposite shoulder. One possible action arising out of the application is to sweep the opponent's front foot either inwards or outwards, as shown.

Alternatively, the opponent's leg can be reaped. In an inwards sweep, for example, the leg can hit the opponent's sensitive point Spleen 6, causing instability in the inner ligament of the leg. This can be followed by a variety of countering techniques as desired. By using this combination, or opening, Shotokan Karate illustrates the principle of a direct, mostly hard style of combat, in keeping with the philosophy of Shaolin Kempo.

Warding off   *Foot reap Remove*

Arm lock

Kouchi Gaeri, throw

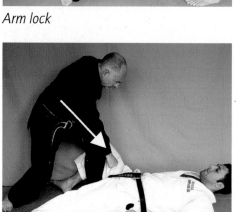

Closing technique

It is somewhat different in Goju Ryu. The front leg is moved towards the opposite shoulder, aimed more at an escape action as in Tai Sabaki than at a direct opening as in Shotokan.

Warding off and countering movements come out of a 45° position, as demonstrated. So seen, this combat style is different in that it tends to combine hard and soft. The opening, once again, offers numerous variations of countering techniques.

Repositioning the front leg

Warding off

Countering technique

1.5.4   Chudan Attack Becomes Jodan

Attacks in the Shotokan Kata, e.g. in Shuri Te, are preferably carried out at the level of Chudan (stomach level). The style of the combinations, however, tells us that most of the attacks are executed at Jodan (head) level and not at Chudan. The result of this is that the opponent uses a defensive movement which moves his head down to medium height (Chudan).

This can be seen in the following illustrations of the combinations Osae Uke, Nukite. More information about other Kata can be found in publications which detail the interpretation of the individual Kata.

Gripping the wrist

Osae Uke brings the opponent to Chudan Level

Nukite to Conception Vessel 22 (CV22)

Sensitive point directly on the windpipe

1.5.5 The Particularities of Shuto Uke

We need to free ourselves of the idea that Shuto Uke in the Kata is only to be interpreted as "defense". Let us remember Funakoshi's remark: "Every defense is also an attack." On the surface of things it may seem incomprehensible that when using this technique the rear open hand lands at the height of one's own solar plexus. If the rear hand were to be withdrawn back to the hip after grabbing the opponent's sleeve or wrist, as is normally practiced, and as shown in the following pictures, we would then have a situation where the distance is no longer suitable for a strike with the side of the hand against the carotid artery (Stomach 9, ST9). It is only when the rear hand is actually withdrawn to the solar plexus, and turned, that the opponent is opened up and we have the correct distance for a hit to the neck.

 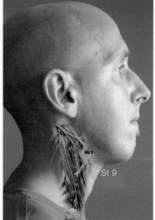 

Incorrect Shuto application   *Correct*

1.5.6 The Preparatory Hand in a Block

Another easily overseen detail is the "preparatory" hand in the Shuto Uke technique. Regardless of whether an opponent uses his left or his right hand to start an attack, the defender can choose to use either his right or left hand to repulse it. The defending movement can take the form of either a sweeping block (Nagashi Uke) or a bumping block (Teisho Uke).

This combination in the Kata is extremely clever as it makes no difference whether the attack comes from the right fist or the left, though this may not be immediately obvious in practice; the following illustrations show both the left and the right version.

Defense and counter in an attack from the right

Defense and counter in an attack from the left

1.5.7 Turning the Front and Rear Fist

Turning the rear fist

In the Kata and in elementary schooling the rear fist is usually turned back to the hip. The purpose of this is twofold: to increase the advancing speed of the front hand or fist and to grip an opponent so he can be put off balance by pulling and twisting his hand. This disruption of the opponent's balance (Kuzushi) is an important principle of the Martial Arts.

Gripping the wrist   *Counter grip and twist*   *Pulling back to hip and disturbing balance*

Using both hands

The principle of bringing the opponent out of balance is even clearer with the correct use of both hands. It makes an opening for easier locking and throwing.

Gripping both wrists   *Holding and twisting the opponent's wrist*   *Pulling and turning the opponent*

Turning the front fist

Turning the front fist 45° gives stability to the forearm bone, which is excellently supported by the ligament and muscle apparatus. Turning further to 90°, as is usual in Karate, results in the ulna and the radius bones being turned over one another. The static of the bones is worsened by the complete twist, but this is compensated for by increased muscle tension. Looking at the form of the ribcage opening we can see that it would be most difficult for the whole turned fist to slip through the arches of the ribs to reach the plexus. Therefore, the fist is turned horizontally only after passing rib arch level. A maximum effect can be achieved by turning the fist in the body and slightly downward directly on the solar plexus. . The angle of the hit being delivered in an attack or counter determines the effectiveness of the hit. Moreover, the most effective angle to be chosen depends on the area or organ targeted: straight ahead for the spinal column, upwards for the diaphragm, lung, or heart, or downwards for the pelvic organs.

Turning the fist back at the hip

Fist hitting at 45°

Screwing the fist in after passing the rib arches

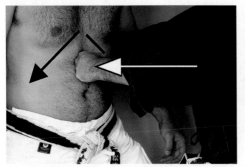

Fist hitting between the rib arches

Screwing the fist into the Solar Plexus

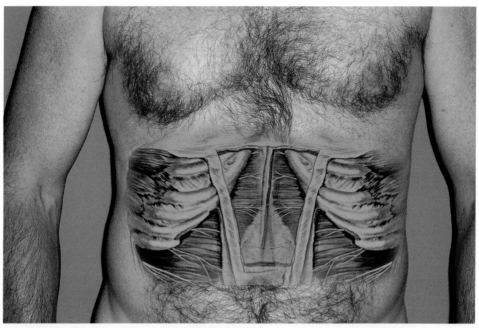

Configuration of the rib arches on the surface

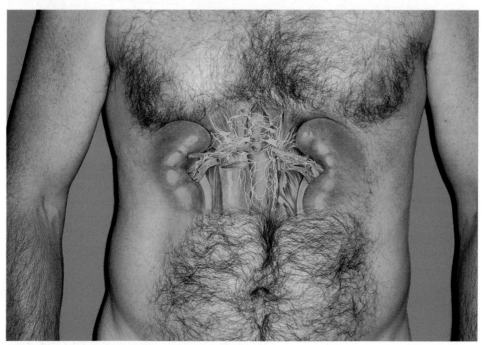

Anatomical seat of the solar plexus, at depth, in front of the spinal column

1.5.8   Each and Every Block is an Attack

A number of examples will demonstrate that every defense is simultaneously an attack. The following shows the Age Uke block giving rise to an Age Uchi strike. The decisive factor is that the preparatory hand is in control (e.g. with Nagashi Uke, Teisho or Tate).

Age Uchi to the neck (CV 23)   *Age Uchi to the armpit (Heart 1, He 1)*

The typical forearm block from outside to the inside, i.e. the Soto Ude Uke, is used as a punch. The forearm or the metacarpus small head of the 5th finger is used to strike sensitive points on the opponent's arm or head. This affects the opponent's body in such a way that a hit to further points could result in a knock out, or could paralyze the arm.

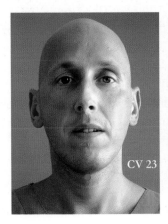

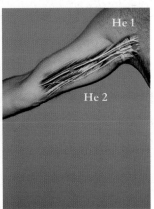

Soto Uke/Uchi

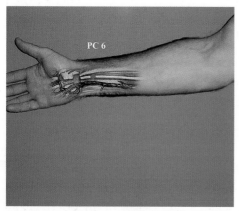

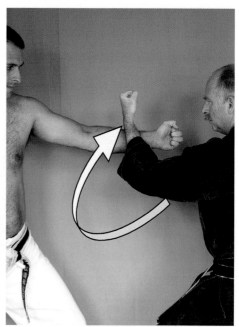

Pericard 6 (Kyusho sensitive point). Hits change regulation of the circulatory system

Hit to PC 6 by either the forearm or the metacarpus of the 5th finger

Uchi Uke as a lock

Sensitive Kyusho points can also be used in locks to increase their effect. It is universally accepted that Uchi Ude Uke cannot be used in a free fight, whereas variations of this block are definitely meaningful in close combat applications. A hit to the acupuncture point Lung 6 will cause the opponent's arm to be so weakened that an opening for a lock becomes significantly easier. This Kyusho point also has a "conditioning" effect on heart and circulatory point sensitivity in the neck and on the ribcage. Just a powerful block with the fingers to Lung 6 causes the opponent to bend his arm and his front leg to buckle. Other sensitive points on the upper arm can be effectively used in the application of various levers. The hammer lock entry is a good illustration of this.

Straight fist stab

Entry by Uchi Uke to Lung 6

Moved into Large Intestine 13 on the upper arm

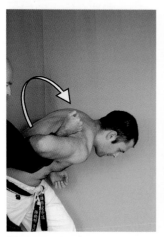

Hammer Lock

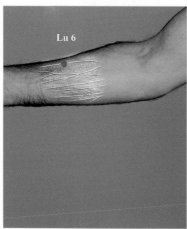

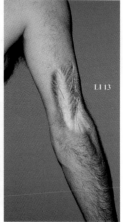

Anatomical co-relationship of nerves at Lung 6 and Large Intestine 13

Gedan Barai/Uchi

Once again, the downwards forearm block needs to do more than merely block; it needs to attack sensitive points to achieve its full effect. It is quite unrealistic to believe this block could withstand a kick. Without deflecting (Tai Sabaki) and without a hit to sensitive points one can only invite injury by relying purely on the use of power, and in the end impede one's own ability to act. It is important to have a weak point in mind with every block, and to hit it. The following show the forearm block in the direction of Spleen 6 and Liver 9. These hits are capable of effectively weakening the opponent's leg and of causing numbness and intense pain.

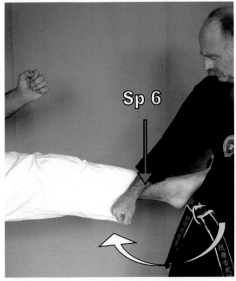

Forearm block to Spleen 6 (Sp 6)

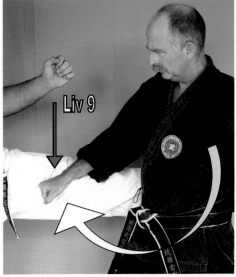

Forearm block with the small finger small head to Liver 9 (Liv 9)

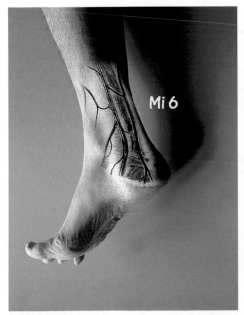

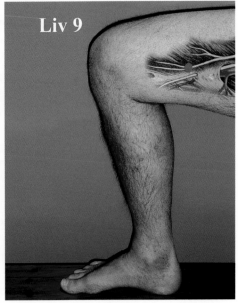

Anatomical reference of acupuncture points to nerves and vessels

Nagashi Uke/Uchi

Using the soft block as a sweep can also achieve more effectiveness in its numerous variations when combined with weak points. Again, it is not just force which leads to the success of a defensive technique, but also the appropriate angle and the

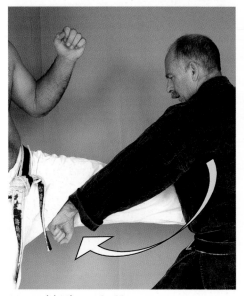

Nagashi Uke to Sp11

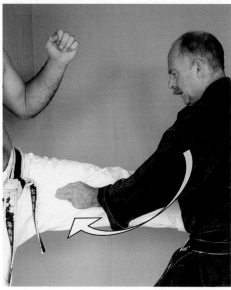

Finger stab to Sp11

utilization of the Kyusho points. The following shows Nagashi Uke being used to hit Spleen 11 (Sp 11) on the inside of the thigh. The leg is weakened by intense pain when certain nerve tracts are hit. This simultaneously increases the sensitivity of other meridians such as the stomach, for example, making it easier to achieve a KO.

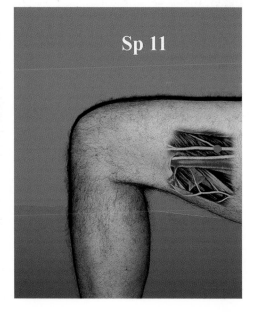

Anatomical reference for Sp11

Juji Uke/Uchi

Juji Uke as an arm block

Juji Uke as an attack to the neck (St 9)

The cross-block allows the arm easier entry to locks to the inside and to the outside as described in the Chapter 1.7 "Levers". In its application as an attack to the neck, the metacarpus of the small finger strikes above Stomach 9 (St 9, branching of carotid artery), an active circulatory Kyusho point. Activating the nerve bundles for tension measurement on the carotid artery means that the body is fed false information. The circulatory controls receive the message that blood pressure is too high, causing a counter regulating massive drop in blood pressure. The result is un-consciousness or, at the least, a dazed state. The technique is equally effective

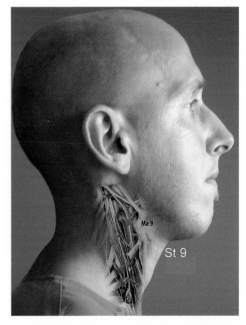

Juji Uke with the open hand

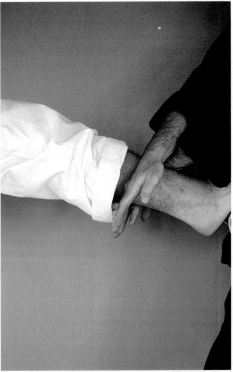

Juji Uke, strike to Spleen 6 (Sp 6)

using open hands. The cross-block is a basic technique in many Kata. The combinations with other techniques depend on the individual Kata. This will be explained further in later chapters.

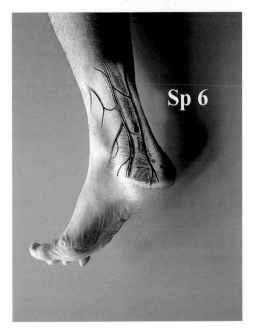

Sp 6

Hidari Jodan Haiwan Uke, Migi Ude Soete

This double block may not appear suitable for realistic combat at first glance. A different light is put on things, however, when we have a situation of self-defense in close quarters. The closed fists in the block give the impression of intending to grab the opponent's arm. A hit with the right forearm to Large Intestine 13 (opponent's upper arm) weakens the arm for an easier lock as in a sword throw. A backwards shift (Kokutsu Dachi) brings the opponent out of balance.

Block out of Heian Nidan

Weakening the arm and lock, upsetting balance with Kokutsu Dachi

Application as a lock (Ude Garami)

Forearm lock with both hands

Backwards movement

Increasing the forearm lock in submission on the floor, entangled arm lock

Kaishu Haiwan Uke

Application as Ude Garami with open hands

The lock can be applied using either the left or right hand, or both.

Using open hands permits a simultaneous block and strike to neck (St 9).

1.5.9   Kousa Dachi

The cross-step has a substantial role in the Art of Sword and Stick Fighting. As the following shows, Kousa Dachi is not only to be interpreted as an in-between step in unarmed self-defense but also as an application for penetrating low kicks. Sequences from the Naihanchi Kata show the following interpretations:

Cross-step, Kousa Dachi in Naihanchi

Kick to Spleen 6 (SP 6), by raising the opponent's left foot.

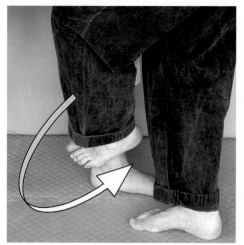

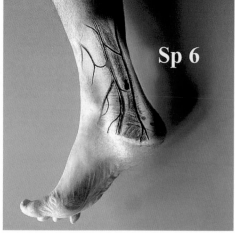

The kick with the side of the foot is applied at an upwards angle of 45°, weakening the opponent's foot in this direction.

1.5.10 How Mae Geri Became Yoko Geri

Over time kicks were changed in various Kata in Shotokan Karate. In the old books written by Funakoshi, one can see (as in Shuri Te) that neither Yoko Geri (side kick) nor kicks at Jodan level were practiced. This can be reconstructed in the Tekki Nidan, Kanku Dai and several other Kata. Comparison with the so-called Koshiki Kata (older Karate forms) gives us more insight into later developments.

According to other sources, Yoko Geri, Mawashi Geri and other kick movements were introduced by Funakoshi's sons, who were attracted by the variety of leg techniques in Taekwondo. These techniques are now considered to underline the sporting and athletic character of Shotokan Karate (including the high Jodan version).

1.6   Multiple Meanings of One Technique and Ground Work (Ne Waza)

The remarkable thing about the Karate techniques in the Kata is that they can very often be applied with different variations. The following should help to explain how this is so.

Examples of techniques in the upright position and on the floor:

Standing	**On the floor**

Juji Uke, as a defense technique

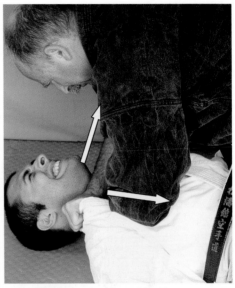

Juji Jime, as a choking technique

Ude Garami, standing

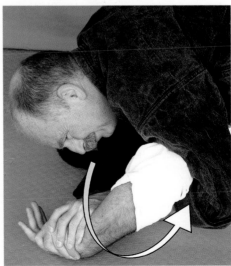

Ude Garami, on the floor

Osae Uke Uraken Uchi (from Tekki)

The following techniques show three different variations of the same movement.

Hit to the chin (CV 24)   *One-handed choking technique, Naked Lock, Hadaka-Jime*   *Two-handed choking technique Variation on Hadaka-Jime*

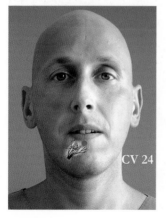

In Uraken CV24 is hit at an angle of 45°

Kousa Dachi

Cross-step (various Kata)   *Cross-choke with the feet, arm lock Ude Higishi Juji Gatame*

This movement (Kousa Dachi) occurs in the starting movement of the Tekki Shodan Kata.

A single technique can be versatile and usually presents us with the possibility of a number of variations. With the following starting movements from the Kata Jion, Jiin or Jitte we can illustrate that a technique really just represents a basic principle which is suitable for multiple applications. In other words, a single technique is not limited to a single use.

Out of the Kata Jion, Jiin, Jitte

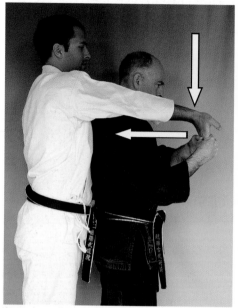

Combination Finger- and Forearm downward press

Wrist joint lock

Reversed wrist press

The same in reverse, Renko Ho, come along technique

Downward reversed wrist joint lock

Elbow downward press

Elbow upward press

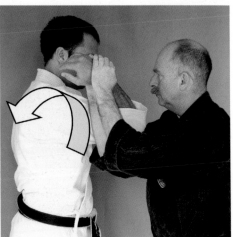

Elbow rear throw (Ude Garami)

Application from the Kata Bassai Dai, Bassai Sho or Kanku Sho

The technique shown here is generally interpreted as Kote Gatame (mentioned in a different part of this book). The following illustrations show a series of variations which reinforce and intensify the lock.

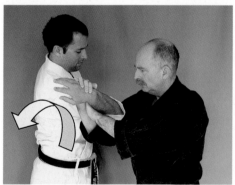

Ude Garami

Elbow rear lock with Kyusho application He 1 Hiji Kujiki Gatame

Arm lock

Modification with additional finger lock

Hammer Lock with neck grip

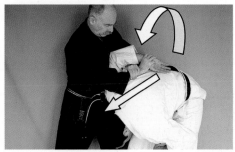

or with wrist grip

Reinforced neck lock

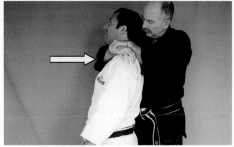

Single-arm choke (Kataha Jime)

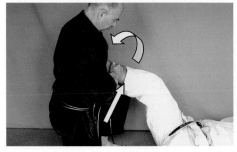

Outward foot lock (Kyusho application Sp 6)

Inward ankle joint lock

1.7 Levers (Tuite, Kansetsu Waza)

uite applications come from Chin Na and are found in numerous Martial Arts. These techniques for twisting joints are, in the majority of cases, reinforced by the utilization of weak (pressure) points for greater effectiveness. Not surprisingly, they are also prevalent in the Kata.

Kote Gatame

The use of this lock not only mechanically weakens the wrist, but also intensifies its effect through the utilization of the acupuncture points Heart 7 and Heart 6 (H 6, H 7) on the ulna-side channel of the wrist. The lock is applied with a cross-grip to the wrist.

Twisting the forearm away from the defender (similar to throttling the fuel flow on a motorbike) enables a correctly angled action which will bring an opponent to his knees (angle 30-45° at the wrist, 90° at the elbow joint, 180° in the shoulder).

Ude Garami

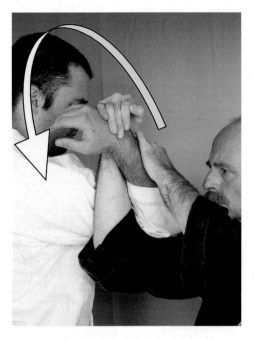

We already know the elbow rear throw. It can be found in the Heian Nidan, Heian Yondan, and in the Jion, Jiin and Jitte Kata, among others. Modifying the angle allows a variation which lies between an elbow rear throw and a sword throw (Uchi Tenkai Nage). A rearwards change of position in Kokutsu Dachi, for example, causes the opponent to lose his balance.

The elbow rear throw (e.g. in Heian Nidan) can be carried out with either the right or the left hand and is equally effective in both cases. It can also be used with both hands, should the opponent be particularly powerful.

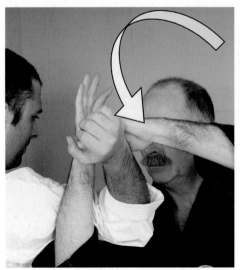

Using the left hand

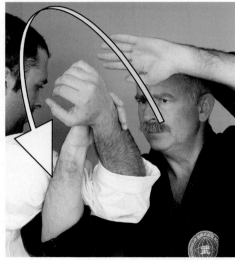

Using the right hand

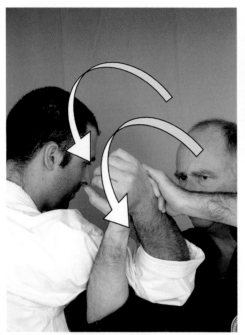

Using both hands

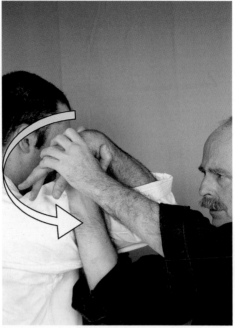

Use of Kyusho Points (TW3, LI13) for Uchi Tenkai Nage (sword throw)

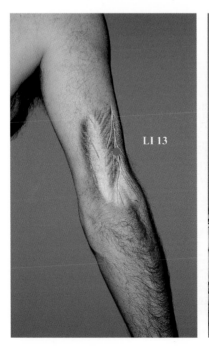

LI 13

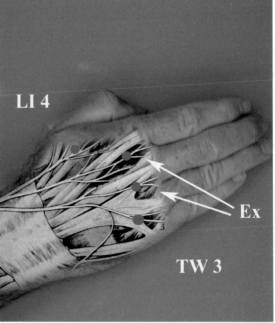

LI 4

Ex

TW 3

Juji Uke

One variation of the cross block includes a typical Tuite. The hand is gripped and the opponent's radius stimulated by rubbing, which causes intense pain. The opponent can quickly be brought under control with the effectiveness of this lever.

Gripping

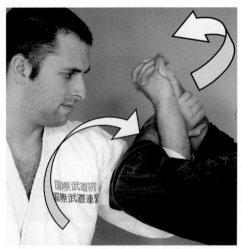

Rubbing the radius with the forearm and lock

Opening to Hammer Lock

Heian Sandan

Change

The opening for a hammer lock with the aid of Kyusho points can be reconstructed from the Heian Sandan Kata. A strike to the Kyusho point Heart 2 (He 2) on the inside of the upper arm can be executed with the distal joint of the thumb neads space spike (Ippon ken) or with the blood pool hand or crest hand (Keito). This causes electrification and paralysis of the entire arm, creating an easy opening for the hammer lock over the Large Intestine 13 (Liv 13). This could actually be a further development of a Kata technique.

Hit to He 2

Entry to lock

Lock over LI 13

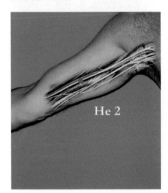

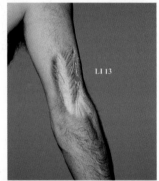

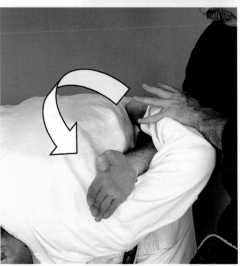

Shuto used to pressure LI 13, giving control over the opponent

Teisho

Depending on the Kata, the Teisho technique can be executed either quickly or slowly. The fast version is a strike (parry) and the use of Kyusho points (e.g. Naihanchi) whereas the slow version includes an escape movement (e.g. Bassai Dai) and incorporates the use of sensitive points to make the technique effective. In other words, the slow movement is an escape lock; the fast technique consists of a strike to weak points on the head or neck, for example.

Teisho from Tekki, or Naihanchi

Teisho with pressure to the larynx and carotid artery (St 9), using knee to put pressure on the back of the opponent's knee at the level of Bladder 40 (Bl 40)

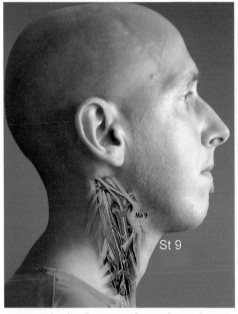

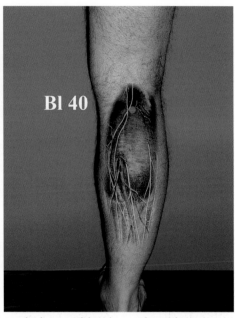

Anatomical reference of Kyusho points St 9 and Bl 40 to blood vessels and nerves.

Wrist joint twist lock from Seifa or Tekki Nidan

Pressure points on the ulna side of the opponent's wrist (He 5 to 7) can be used to facilitate twisting the arm and achieving a wrist joint lock.

Gripping the wrist

Gripping the opponent's wrist with pressure on He 5 to 7

Turning the body, bending the wrist and using the elbow to put pressure on the opponent's elbow

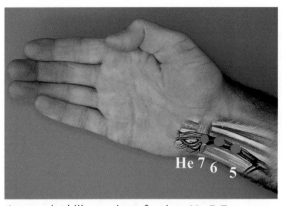

Anatomical illustration of points He 5-7

The differing techniques show us that combinations can be arbitrarily used at will. Taking the last illustration above, for example, we could choose to slip the right knee into the back of the opponent's knee in the closing position in Shiko Dachi to concentrate pressure on the acupuncture point Bladder 40 (see Teisho technique). Intensifying the lock by employing the body (Waki Gatame) is another variation drawn from other Kata. It is a typical example of the fact that the Kata movements should not be seen as static but as flexible in their use.

The following are differing interpretations of a starting movement from the Nijushiho Kata.

The starting movement of the Nijushiho Kata is another example of the versatility of one single movement.

From the Nijushiho Kata

Gripping the wrist (Katate Dori)

Arm lock (Ude Osae), causing the elbow to break

Clinch from behind (Ushiro Kakai Dori)

Escape using Ushiro Enpi and Zenpo Enpi Uchi

It is essential here to ensure that the right shoulder is raised and the left shoulder lowered. Simultaneously, the hips butt into the opponent's genital region and the left elbow is rammed into the short ribs, thereby attacking various Kyusho points. Other applications show the same Nijushiho Kata movement in a different light, as shown in the following examples.

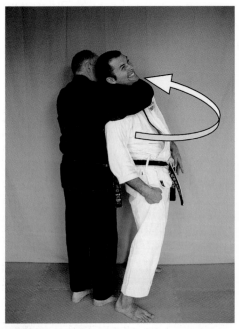

Choking with Kataha Jime, grip on opponent's left arm or pressure on Bladder 23 on the back by Ippon Ken can increase the effectiveness of the choking technique.

Zenpo Enpi Uchi, the opponent's wrist can also be taken in a grip by the left hand.

Lock

The following is a description of a selection of additional lock techniques which can be found in numerous Kata. We will begin by looking at techniques from the Heian Kata, which contain techniques and sequences out of the higher Kata. The starting sequences of the Heian Yondon and Heian Nidan Kata are most likely related to one another. Below is a sequence in Heian Yondan with open hands and in Heian Nidan with the fists closed.

Heian Yondan

Heian Nidan

Defending against a fist attack

Placing a lock over Di 13

Gripping the forearm

Shifting weight (Kokutsu Dachi) to the rear and upsetting the opponent's balance

The lock can be applied using either the left or the right hand, or both hands

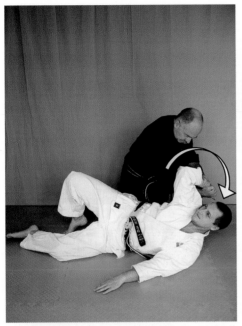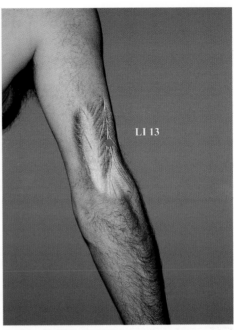

Continuation of elbow rear throw Ude Garami in submission on the floor, entangled arm lock. Pressure to Large Intestine 13

The hands are held open in defense against this type of fist attack, as in HeianYondan; they are closed to form a fist after gripping the opponent's arm. There are most certainly other applications which can be interpreted through the Kata. The most important thing, from our point of view, is that both hands be used effectively. Another example of a possible variation is that the left hand defends while the right hand prepares to launch an attack to the opponent's neck or head. In a reversed position, both hands could divert from the rear side of the forearm and upper arm so that an arm lock could be applied with the appropriate gripping movement. These techniques in the Heian Nidan and Heian Yondan Kata have both a right and a left version. Most Kata have a right and a left version. Changing over from the right to the left position also facilitates the use of effective locks. We can see that these opening sequences of the Kata offer numerous techniques and possibilities.

Seienchin

Examples of more levers are shown using the Seienchin Kata. Various descriptions of different Bunkai have been referred by other authors.

Sequence from the Kata

Mai Geri, Block, foot lock to the outside

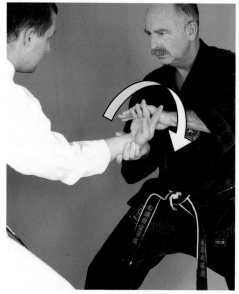

Angle hand lock (Kote Gaeshi)

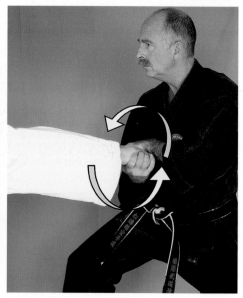

Foot lock to the inside

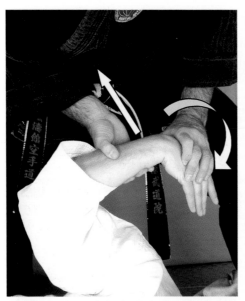

Continuation of the lock in floor position with the help of Kyusho points

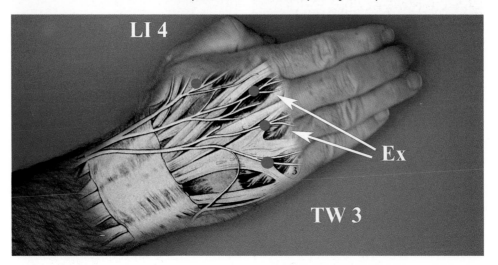

The two abovementioned variations on the application have been described for the same sequence from the Seienchin Kata. Another alternative would be to use a head lock. The Seienchin Kata from Goju Ryu contains an abundance of different escape techniques. These can also be found in the Shotokan Kata, but to a lesser extent. Practically all applications of this kata were developed for close combat. It includes both hard and soft elements and is, therefore, a Kata typically for advanced students, even though the movement sequence does not seem particularly difficult.

Nujushiho

Nijushiho (meaning 24 steps in Japanese) is another Kata which probably originated in Quanfa, in the South. As mentioned before, the opening movement has some similarity to the special sequences of other Kata like Seienchin. Let us take a look at a typical leg lock, which can also be found in the Wankan Kata. Further, there is a similarity to be found between Ni Ju Shi Ho and Ni Ju Hachi Ho (meaning: 28 steps). The Chinese name is Ni Pai Po (also 28 steps), but this Kata differs from Ni Ju Hachi ho.

Sequence from the Nijushiho Kata, Sweeping block

Counter grip to shinbone

Detailed photograph

Application: Sweeping the foot from the left

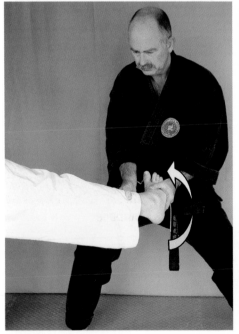

Blocking the shinbone

Foot lock to the inside

Or: Gripping and blocking the leg

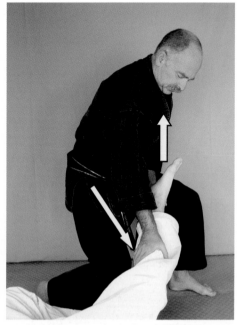

Locking the knee by using pressure on the inner side

Wankan

Here we have a similar technique in the Wankan Kata. This is a very old Kata with only one Kiai.

Sequence from the Kata Wankan, Sweeping block (Nagashi Uke), Blocking the shinbone

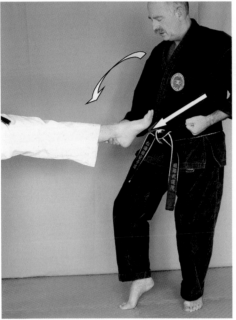

Application: Sweeping block

Inside knee lock

Applying weight to the outside knee ligament. Once the opponent has been thrown, other lock techniques to the foot joint can be used.

Enpi

A leg lock can be developed from the sequence shown in the Kata Enpi.

Sequence from the Kata, preparation

Downward block

Sweeping block

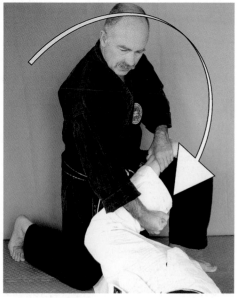

Downward strike to Gb 34

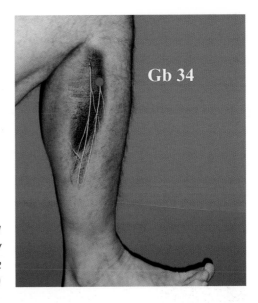

Gb 34

Sweeping block of Mai Geri, entering and changing the angle of attack, blow and lock on the calf bone (Gallbladder 34, Gb 34)

Jion, Jiin, Jitte, Chinte

The downward elbow press described here can be found in different Kata mentioned above.

Sequence from the Jion Kata

Downward elbow press over the shoulder

In the Chinte Kata, the lock can be intensified by hopping backwards.

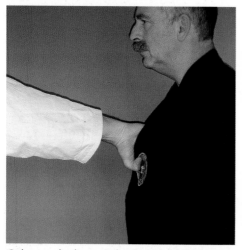

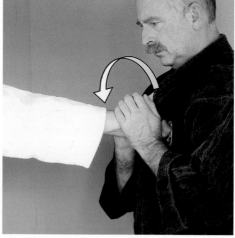

Other variations: Gripping the lapel

Tilting the wrist joint to the ulna

Sochin

The Sochin Kata also contains joint lock techniques.

Sequence from the Kata: Block and attack

Turn with Fumikomi, Gedan Barai, Age Uke

Phase 1: Block and attack to Gb 1, Pitched or TW23, temple with a right Soto Uchi kick (Fumi Komi) to knee, Soto Uchi

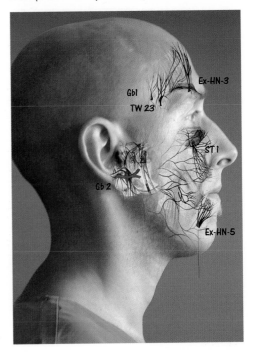

Anatomical reference of the Kyusho points to nerves and vessels

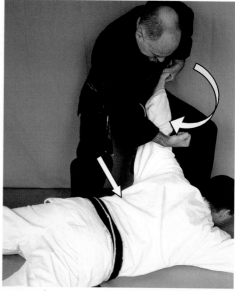

Executed as a lock at the elbow joint (TW 11 or 12), i.e. with Gedan Barai knee to Bl 40

Continuation of arm lock on floor and a knee lock to the attacker's knee

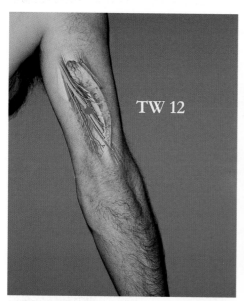

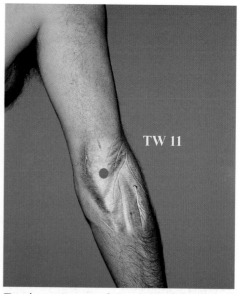

TW 12

TW 11

Interception point of the Nervus radialis

Tension receptor of the triceps tendon

Lock to TW 12 or TW 11(Triple Warmer 11 or 12)

Tekki Nidan (Naihanchi 2)

As we have already mentioned, the Naihanchi Kata contains numerous techniques for self-defense in close quarters. Here is another example of the Tekki Nidan Kata.

Sequence out of the Kata

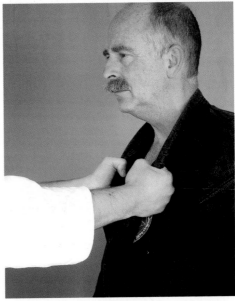

Double-sided grip to lapel

The next sequence from the Kata

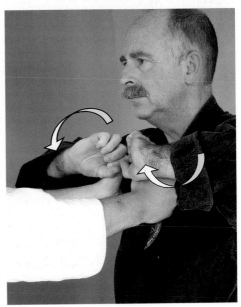

Gripping the thumbs

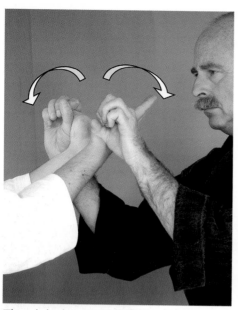

Thumb lock to the outside

Hiza Geri directed at the genital area

Tekki Nidan (Naihanchi 2)

Once again, a lock combination from Tekki Nidan is shown which can also be found in other Kata.

Sequence from the Kata

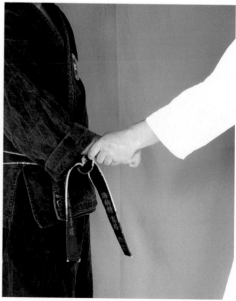

Gripping the wrist joint

Gripping and twisting the opponent's hand (Kote Gatame is also possible)

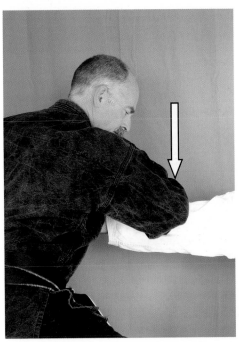

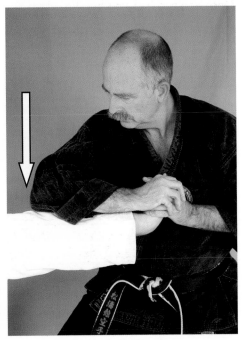

Elbow joint lock, using one's own elbow to apply a downward elbow press.

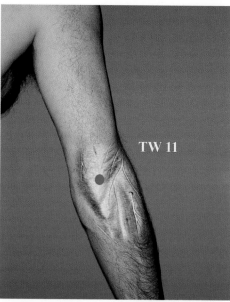

TW 11

Continuation of the elbow press in submission on the floor stimulating the Kyusho point TW 11 (Triple Warmer). A reversed wrist press, aided by Large Intestine 4 (LI 4), can also be used as a reinforcing action. Reference here is to the next sequence in the Kage Tsuki.

Blocking a fist attack

Kage Tsuki as a lock (sensitive point TW 11)

Jion, Jiin, Kanku Sho, Bassai Sho

The above Kata all share the Manji Gamae technique. The following illustrates one variation of the application.

Sequence from the Kata

Neck lock

Closing movement to submission on the floor

Heian Sandan

The Kata Heian Sandan is used (again) to show details of entry to a cross-grip.

Sequence from the Kata

Changing hands

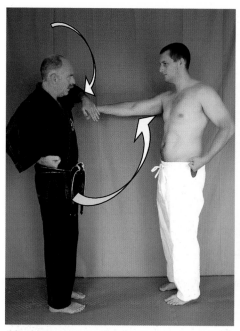

Blocking an attack

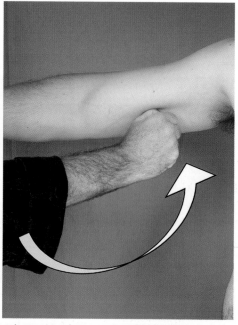

Hit to vessel-nerve sheaf in He 2

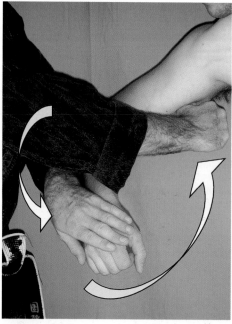

Entry to lock

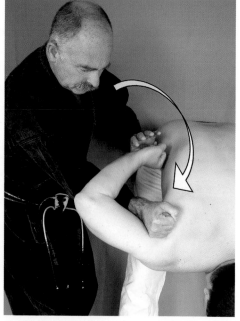

Applying pressure to Large Intestine 13 from the right

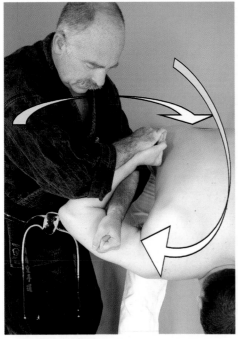

or from the left

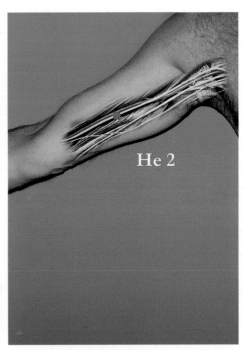

He 2

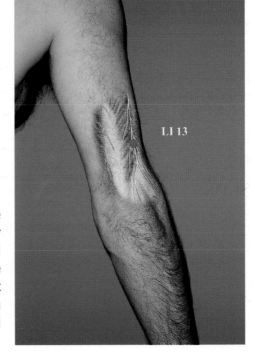

LI 13

As has been mentioned, a hit to the inner vessel-nerve sheaf on the upper arm has the effect of electrifying and paralyzing the entire arm, so that the lock can be carried out without difficulty. A hit to the head, or Gedan Uchi, can follow from the Gedan Barai (or downward block).

1.8   Escape Techniques (Gedatsuho)

Nijushiho

There are two elements in the Kata's opening movement: the Age Empi to the left and the Ushiro Empi to the right.

Front view of the opening movement

Side view

Escape by raising the elbow, lowering the opposite shoulder, Ushiro Empi and simultaneously driving the hip into the opponent's genital region. A similar application also exists in the Goju Ryu Kata Seienchin. The movement goes back to the Drunken Monkey technique.

Hangetsu

This Kata is a defensive movement and is shown here in the Kake form in the Gyaku position.

Front view

Side view

Cross-grip to the wrist

Kake and Kote Gatame

Opening to the downward elbow press

Kanku Dai

We have already been introduced to escape techniques in this Kata.

Movement from the Kata

Converting the hand to a fork

Escape by first weakening and then taking hold of the opponent's wrist.

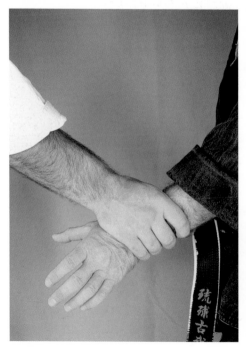

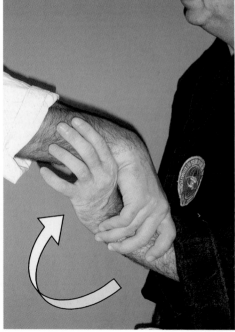

Bassai Dai

In the opening movement of this Kata, the hand slides from the fist to the forearm with a long leap forward into the Kousa Dachi position.

Opening movement

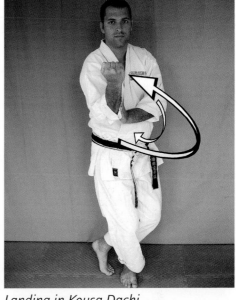

Landing in Kousa Dachi

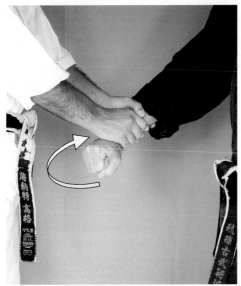

Gripping the wrist with both hands

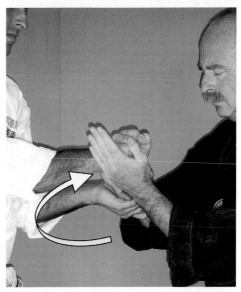

Escape by supporting the fist with the open hand

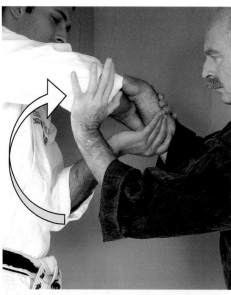

Transition to the downward elbow press

Either mechanically with pressure on the elbow joint

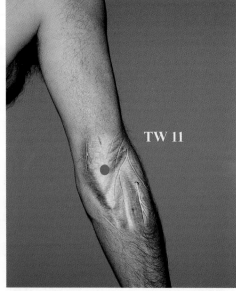

TW 11

or by stimulating the stretching apparatus in front of the elbow and utilizing the Kyusho point Triple Warmer 11 (TW 11). The fist puts pressure on the triceps extensor by way of the ulna in the direction of the lower arm, as if knocking on a door. The resulting pain and the false information received by the stretching apparatus causes the body to yield immediately.

Tekki Nidan

An escape technique from the Tekki Nidan Kata consisting of a closed fist and an open hand (related to a movement from the Seifa Kata)

From the Tekki Nidan Kata with sudden backward movement towards the opposite hip

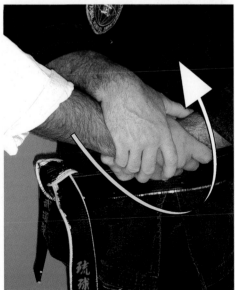

A grip to the wrist on the same side   *Taking hold of the opponent's wrist*

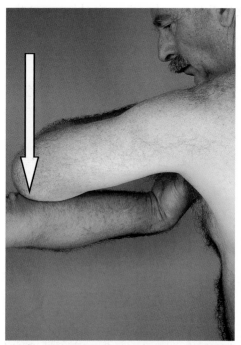

Sudden forward jerk to the opponent's hand, a blow or pressure from the elbow to the stretching apparatus of the opponent's triceps tendon (TW 11)

Front view of the same technique which causes the opponent to bend over. Movements with a powerful jerk can break the wrist and elbow joints.

Another interesting detail explains why both fists are placed on the hip: when the wrist has been gripped on the same side, the opponent's hand is grasped and first pulled to the hip on the same side. Next, it is wrenched with a jerk to the opposite hip, confusing the opponent's defense reflexes.

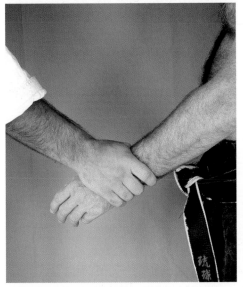

Gripping the wrist

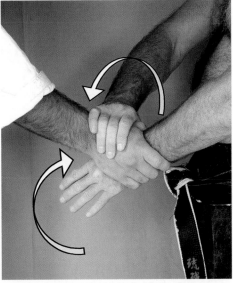

Taking hold of the opponent's wrist

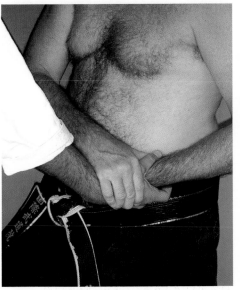

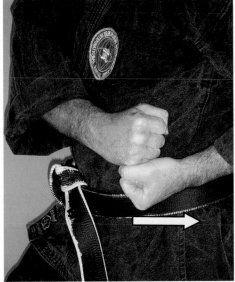

Taking control of the opponent by pulling his hand to the hip. This explains the position "fist on fist" on the hip.

Tensho

This Goju Ryu Kata has a number of varying escape techniques, some of which can be found in Shotokan Kata. The Tensho Kata sequence is, however, exemplary.

Repeated Kake

Raising the hand as in Kakuto

Lowering the hand as in Teisho

Sideways movement of the hand as in Kakuto

Inward withdrawal
of the hand with Teisho

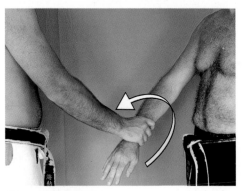

Cross-grip to wrist

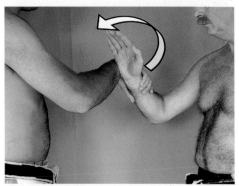

Escape by means of Kake

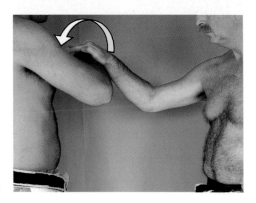

*And gripping
the opposing wrist*

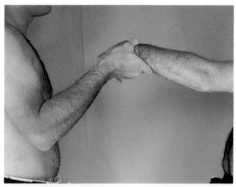
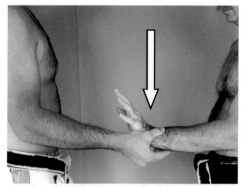

Gripping the wrist, escape by moving the wrist up and down

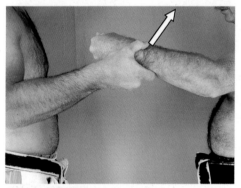
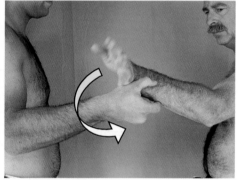

Or to the inside   *and the outside*

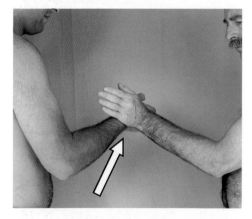

*Deflecting the wrist
again to the inside*

These are movements which copy the flipper movements of a fish. The most important aspect is that this is a soft movement, maintaining the Goju Ryu philosophy of meeting a hard action (in this case, firm grip to the wrist) with a soft defensive movement.

Bassai Dai, Bassai Sho, Kanku Sho

Another escape action to be found in the abovementioned Kata is the Kote Gatame technique. This refers to a particularly painful twist of the wrist.

Front view of the movement from the Kata

Side view

The direction of movement has to be changed in this application. This means feigning a step to the side and then slightly forward to twist the wrist at the correct angle. The wrist should be twisted 30° to 45°, the elbow bent up to 90° and the

shoulder splayed up to 180°. Lowering the body and twisting the lower arm results in extreme pain for the opponent and causes him to sink to his knees. Without the correct angle, however, the lock will be too weak.

We must remember that the Kata movements have to be correctly practiced thousands of times for them to be effectively applied in real situations. We also need to remember that not all aspects or movements of the Kata are taught to everyone. For instance, the deceptive moves of the kata illustrated above are not described in Kote Gatame. This means that the Okuden techniques remain hidden to the less experienced and to the uninitiated.

It takes a very long time to correctly execute and perfect techniques of this sort, especially without guidance. Instruction and direct guidance from an experienced Master still remains indispensable. Moreover, this book is neither able to nor intended to fully describe all details essential for executing the techniques of a Bunkai.

Tekki (Naihanchi)

This Kata sequence, Tekki 1 to 3, contains numerous techniques for combat at close range which are also valuable for use as escape actions. In the Tekki Shodan Kata, for example, both fists are suddenly moved from one hip to the other, the significance of which is not obvious at first glance.

Phase 1 from Tekki

Shifting the fists

Phase 2, the fists have been placed on the opposite hip. The application now opens up the following possibilities. This could be the starting point of defense against a blow coming from the opponent. In this case, the hand is first grabbed and pulled to the right hip (as in Phase 1). We then utilize a bent-hand lock and jerk the hand over to the left hip. Simultaneously, the right elbow can deal a blow out to the opponent's head.

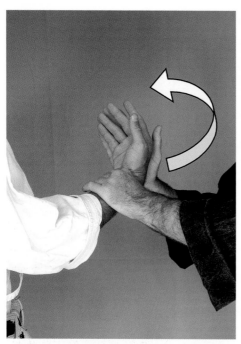

Initiating the bent-hand lock

Jerking movement to the other hip

Intensifying the lock by pressure to Kyusho point TW 3

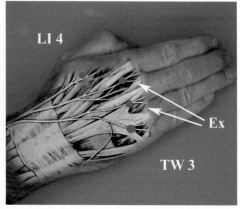

Another technique from the Naihanchi Kata is the movement with Teisho.

Movement from the Kata

Application: clinch from behind

Placement of the right leg behind the opponent, using the right knee to put pressure on the back of the opponent's knee (Bladder 40), while at the same time pushing the opponent over backwards with Teisho (open hand press)

This technique can generally be used against a more powerful opponent. All applications are most effective with the element of surprise (when an opponent is not expecting them or does not know them).

 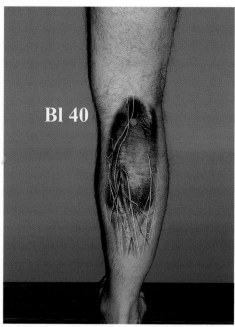

Many follow-up techniques are possible once the opponent has fallen down.

The three forms of the Naihanchi Kata contain numerous attack and defense combinations which are primarily intended for close combat. They represent the Kata most preferred by Choki Motobu, who considered them to be the mainstay of his fighting techniques. Other typical Tekki (Naihanchi) techniques will be shown in other chapters. They include an abundance of various escape techniques such as levers, throws and Kyusho attack techniques. In my opinion this is one of the most important elementary Kata.

Heian Sandan

The closing movement of this Kata shows us additional escape alternatives. We have already seen a similar form in Nijushibo and Seienchin.

Closing movement from the Kata

Clinch from behind

Evasion to the right, Ushiro Empi left backward fist jab to the left

Most vital in the initial movement is the counter movement of the shoulders (the Drunk Monkey)

It is conspicuous that the feigned movement in the Kata Heian Sandan seems to be to the wrong side. However, we cannot say, with any certainty, whether this is due to a translation error or if it is intentionally misleading.

Another sequence from this Kata consists of Osae Uke, Nukite, turning movement, Tetsui

Osae Uke, Nukite

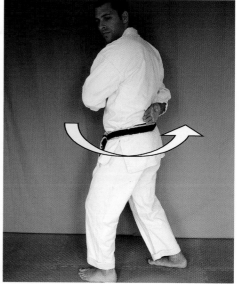

Turning movement

Tetsui

The application is relatively easy to understand and is, therefore, considered one of the Omote techniques.

Gripping the wrist with two hands

Turning movement

Escape, Tetsui

Kanku Dai

There is a similar sequence of movement in the Kanku Dai Kata in which the hand is placed behind the neck in the closing movement, and not behind the back.

Osae Uke, Nukite

Escape, turning movement past the head

Tetsui

The application is similar to the Tekki Sandan although it can be classified as an obvious (Omote) movement.

Gripping the wrist with two hands

Escape and turning movement

For example: a blow with the left elbow to the kidney region, follow with Tetsui

Kururunfa

Another application is found in the Goju Ryu Kata Kururunfa. In a clinch from behind, Ippon Ken is used to stimulate the Extra Points between the metacarpal bones, causing extreme pain and resulting in loosening of the attacker's grip.

Clinch from behind

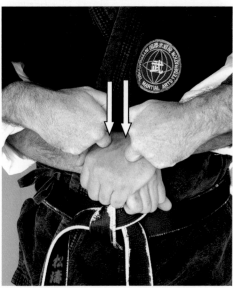

Blow with Ippon Ken to the Extra Points between the metacarpal bones

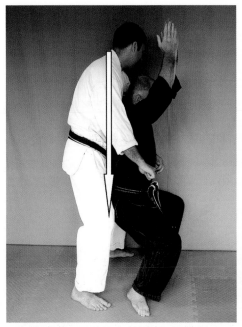
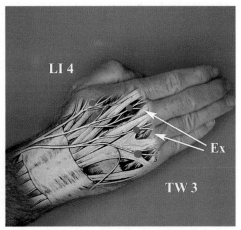

Escape by dropping

The Kata offers numerous applications for escape from a fight in close quarters which are not shown here. Unfortunately, it is not possible to display all of the techniques here as that would most definitely go beyond the scope of this book.

I.9   Sensitive Points (Jintai Kyusho)

Heian Shodan

Kyusho techniques to sensitive points are to be found even in the first Shotokan Kata.

From Gedan Barai

Withdrawing the hand to Tetsui Uchi

Blocking an attack

Drawing back the right leg, Tetsui (Hammer blow) to the side of the chin

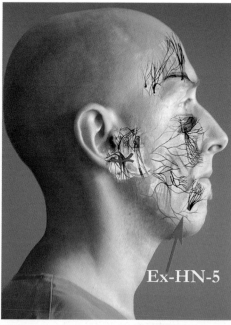

Ex-HN-5

Raising the front foot in the Nekoashi Dachi / Cat Stance increases the effectiveness of a same-sided fist technique

The same technique can be used to escape from a wrist grip.

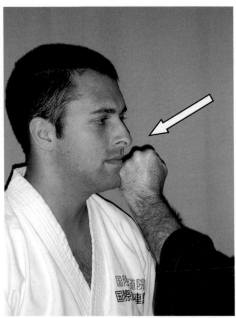

The front foot can remain on the floor for a cross-blow to the opposite corner of the chin.

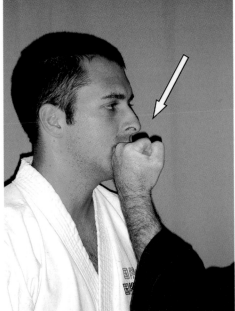

The foot should be raised for a same-sided blow to ensure optimum Qi-flow. This technique can result in a possible knock out.

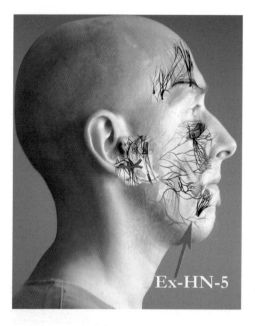

The attack is aimed at an Extra Point on the chin, below the corner of the mouth (EX-HN-5).

Seienchin

This Kata entails a stab to the Notch Region. The stabbing hand is stabilized by the supporting fist below it.

Sequence of the Kata

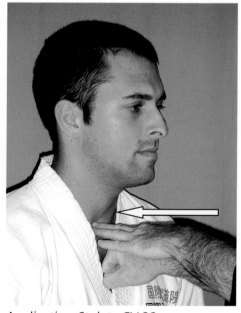

Application: Stab to CV 22

An attack directly towards the windpipe (Conception Vessel 22, CV 22) causes a spasm in the breathing muscles and is extremely dangerous (Warning: Do not experiment with this.). This technique is also to be found in many other Kata, though without reinforcement of the fist. In this case, however, the technique is carried out in a vertical position, not horizontally. The technique shown here is the more effective. It is not known whether or not the technique was deliberately changed in the other Kata.

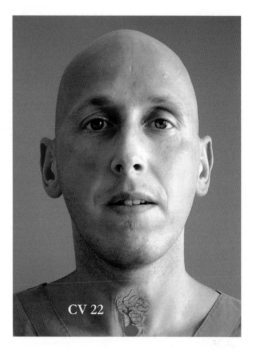

CV 22

Bassai Dai

Seemingly unspectacular blocks can also find sensitive points on the body, as shown in this example with Gyaku Soto Ude Uke to Pericard 6 (PC 6).

Sequence of the Kata

Hit with metacarpal bone V

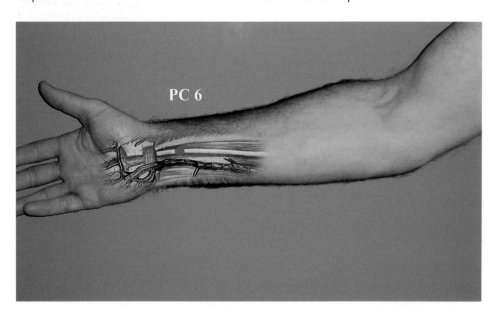

PC 6

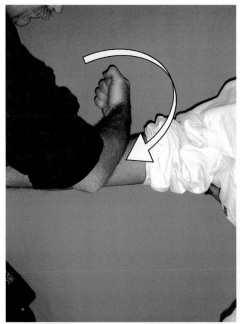

Another variation: Opening to the downward elbow press using Soto Uke with stimulation of the sensitive point TW 11

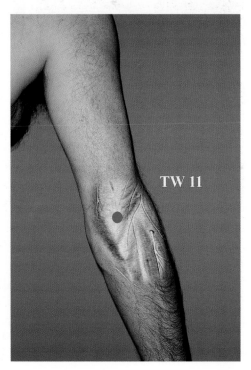

TW 11

Unsu

The first movement of the Kata Unsu (Keito Uke) has a Kyusho application. This is, therefore, not simply a defense movement but rather an attack to the sensitive point Heart 2 (He 2) on the inner side of the upper arm. A blow to this point causes the sensation of an electric shock due to irritation of the nerve and results in paralysis of the arm.

Morote Kaito Uke

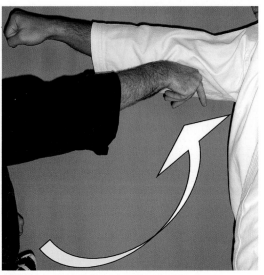

Hit from the Cock's-comb hand to He 2

Side view of the Kata

Hooking-in (Nekoashi), inner foot reap (Ko Uchi Gari) right

Throw with inner reap

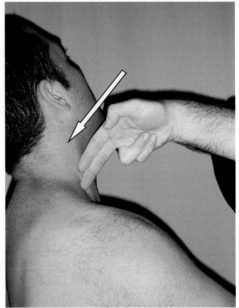

*A stab (Ippon Nukite)
to Large Intestine 18 (LI 18)*

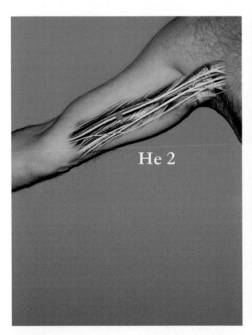

He 2

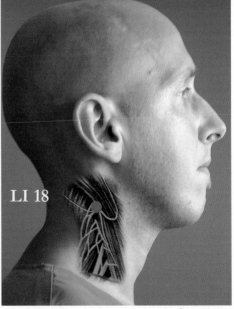

LI 18

A stab to Large Intestine 18 activates the Nervus vagus which causes a dazed feeling or a possible loss of consciousness. The stab can also be directed at the

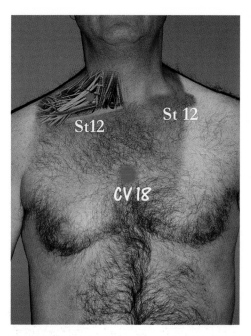

hollow behind the collarbone to affect the vessel-nerve sheaf (Stomach 12, ST 12). This leads to paralysis of the arm, difficulty in breathing and the legs giving way.

Hangetsu

The movement shown is carried out slowly in Hangetsu. It is typical for stimulation of the body's sensitive points.

Out of the Kata: Phase 1

Phase 2

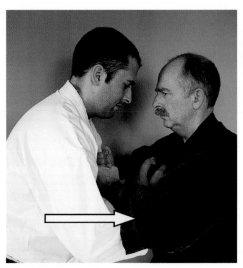

Double-sided grip to the lapels

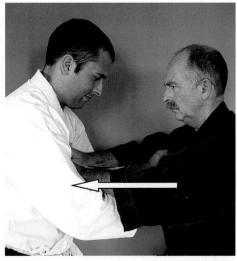

Pressure on the nipples with Ippon Ken

A blow to the nipples, Kyusho point Stomach 17 (St 17), causes intense pain. The pain and nerve impulses coming from a powerful hit can be so strong that loss of consciousness results.

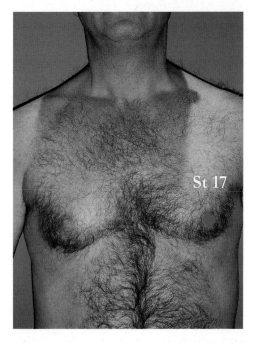

St 17

Chinte

The Chinte Kata offers numerous Kyusho attacks, some of which are described here.

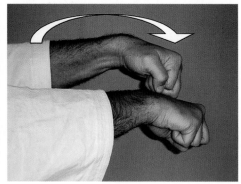

Out of the Kata: Ippon Ken Furi Otoshi.   Nakanada Ippon Ken

The targeted sensitive points are those of the opponent, not one's own.

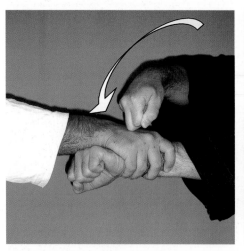

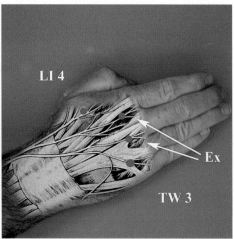

Aim is directed at the Extra Points between the metacarpal bones, or Triple Warmer 3 (TW 3) between the 4th and 5th metacarpal bone. A hit will cause the opponent to loosen his grip immediately. The accompanying pain renders the hand partially useless for a short period of time.

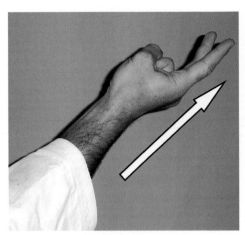
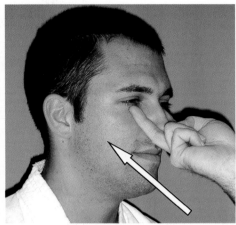

Nihon Nukite Uchi Uke

This technique is directed at the eyes (as in Jodan Nihon Nukite). An alternative is a blow beneath the chin.

The turning movement in Hasami Uchi and Nakadaka Ippon Ken comes after the technique has already been followed through to target the rear.

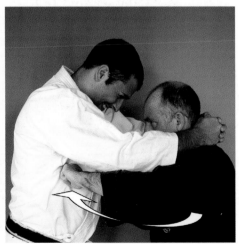

Hasami Uchi Nakadaka Ippon Ken   *Blow to the short ribs, or rib cage*

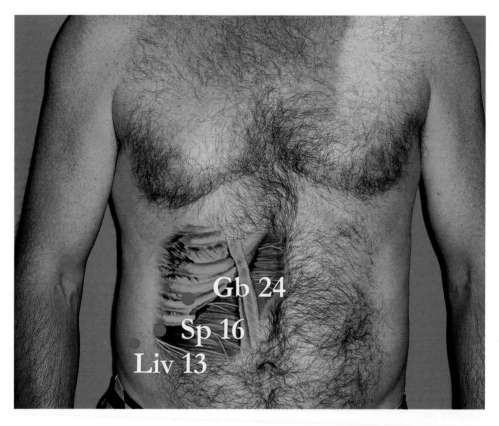

A number of very sensitive Kyusho points are located in the area of the ribcage and the short ribs. These are: Liver 13 (Liv 13), Spleen 16 (Sp 16) and Gall Bladder 24 (Gb 24). A heavy blow to any of these points can result in shortness of breath and loss of consciousness. The short ribs region is, in fact, very vulnerable, as a powerful blow can be dangerous and lead to serious injury of organs such as the spleen and the liver.

Goju Shi Ho Dai

The Washite Age Uchi technique is seldom found in the Kata. Therefore, it is given special attention here.

Washite Age Uchi

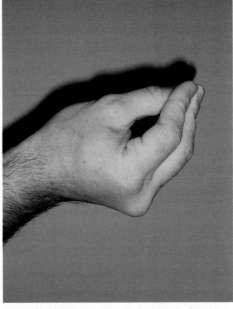

Detailed view

An attack with Age Washite is directed at the tongue bone Conception Vessel 23 (CV 23), a very fragile bone on which the muscles at the base of the mouth and the larynx are hung. This is another point which should not be played around with, as a heavy blow can cause life-threatening bleeding and accompanying danger of suffocation.Even a less powerful hit can cause loss of consciousness due to breathing cramps. The attack is carried out at an upwards angle of 45°.

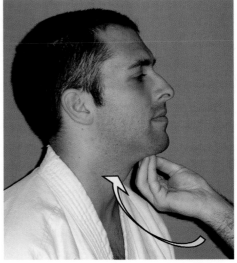

Application: Attack beneath the chin

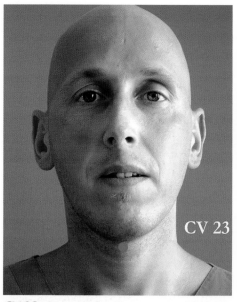

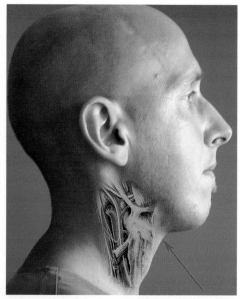

CV 23

CV 23

Tongue bone

Heian Jondan

This Kata is often executed with a grip to the head and a knee blow by raising the knee- once again, the obvious interpretation (Omote). A more subtle technique is a blow to Stomach 9 at the throat (St 9) and to Gall Bladder 20 (Gb 20) at the neck. The sensor for the blood pressure for the carotid artery is under Kyusho point Stomach 9. The large occipital nerve is under Gall Bladder 20 which is directly connected to the brain stem.

Sequence of the Kata: Gripping

and Hiza Geri

Hit to the throat (St 9)

Hit to the neck (Gb 20)

Hiza Geri

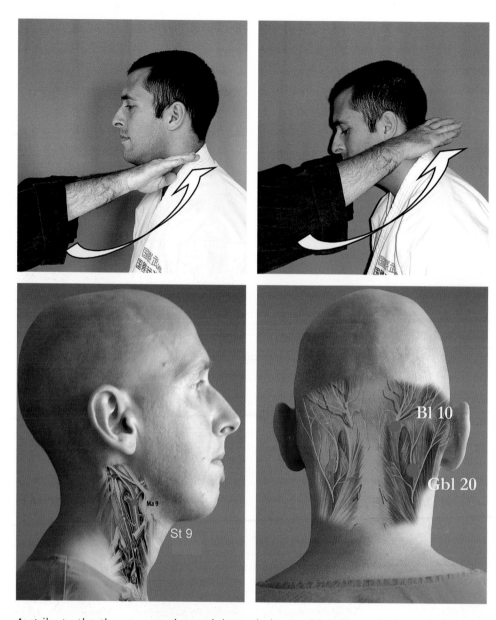

A strike to the throat or to the neck is carried out with Haito, which generally uses the small head of the metacarpal bones to hit sensitive points.

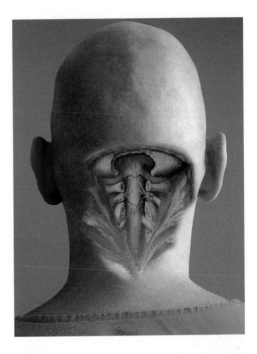

In-depth view of connection to the brain stem

Ni Ju Shi Ho

Haito is a technique which is also used in the Ni Ju Shi Ho Kata in a much more powerful form.

Haito out of the Kata

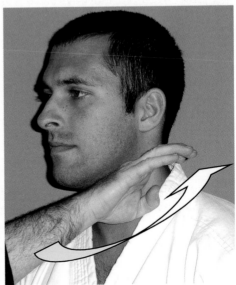

Hit to Stomach 9 (St 9) on the throat

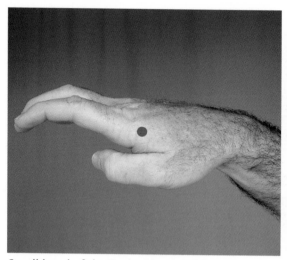 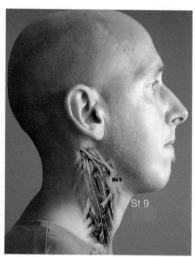

Small head of the 2nd metacarpal bone, which is used to hit St 9

This technique causes dazedness or a possible loss of consciousness should Kyusho point St 9 be hit.

Seienchin

A reverse sequence is found in the closing movement of the Seienchin Kata. Although similar, the hit comes from the rear.

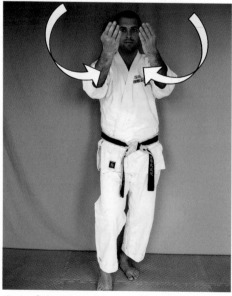 

Out of the Kata: Morote Shuto Phase 1   *Morote Shuto Phase 2*

In the application:

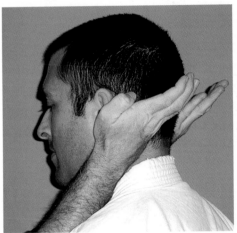
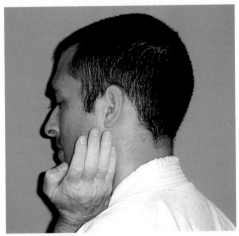

First Shuto-attack to Gall Bladder 20 (Gb 20) Then attack to Stomach 9 (St 9)

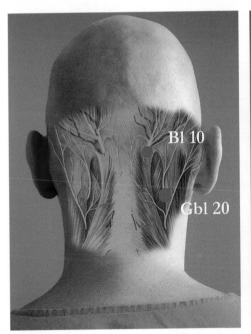
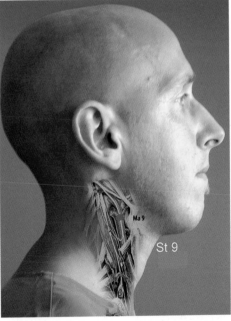

Bl 10

Gbl 20

Ma 9

St 9

An attack to Gb 20 at the back of the head in the direction of the eye (45°) causes shock to the optic nerves, transferred over the large occipital nerve. The result is direct stimulation of the brain stem which can then lead to loss of consciousness or dazedness. Hits to St 9 generally result in a circulatory reaction which can cause a drop in blood pressure, a dazed state, or loss of consciousness.

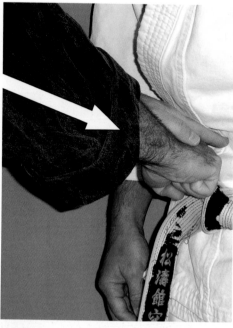

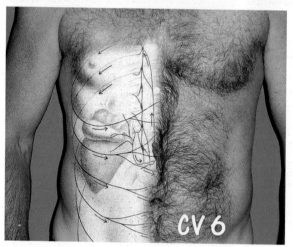

CV 6

The closing movement has already been explained. It refers to a stab in the direction of the Conception Vessel 6 (CV 6), resulting in powerful stimulation of the nerve plexus in the minor pelvis. The stab should be directed downwards at 45°.

Heian Shodan, Heian Nidan, Kanku Dai, Kanku Sho

The use of Shuto has already been described elsewhere in this book. Attack is basically directed at Stomach 9 (St 9).

Out of the Kata: Shuto

The right hand draws the opponent in

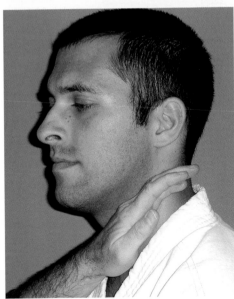

The other hand hits Stomach 9 (St 9)

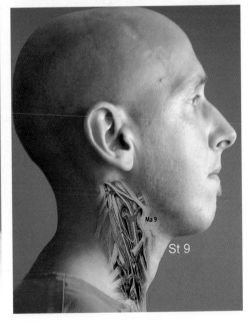

A reminder: Stomach 9 directly influences the circulatory system. A hit results in a drop in blood pressure, causing a dazed state or loss of consciousness.

Tekki (Naihanchi)

In many cases the Tekki Kata often have Uraken from the right or from the left. Uraken attacks can be to the side of the chin below the corner of the mouth (EX-HN-5), higher on the temple, Gall Bladder 1, Triple Warmer 23 or to the Conception Vessel 24 (CV 24). The neurological stimulus causes either a dazed state or a loss of consciousness.

From the Kata: Uraken

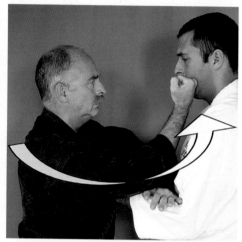

Application to EX-HN-5

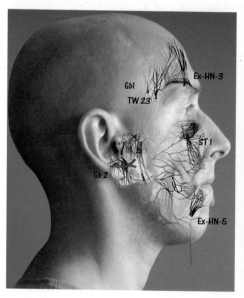

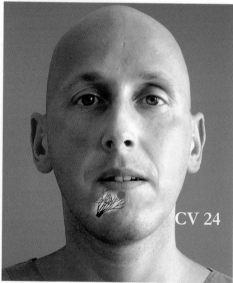

These represent examples of Kyusho points as targets of attack. The Naihanchi Kata contain a number of attack points of this sort.

Heian Yondan, Kanku Dai

The technique is similar in both Kata. The blow is an upwards movement and is aimed at the Conception Vessel or the Governing Vessel in the front middle line. A hit can be dealt to the bridge of the nose (GV 25), base of the nose, upper lip (GV 26, 27, 28) or the chin (CV 24).

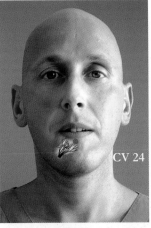

From the Kata: Ura Ken in Kousa Dachi

Application: hit to CV 24

Kyusho point CV 24 with anatomical reference to the facial nerves

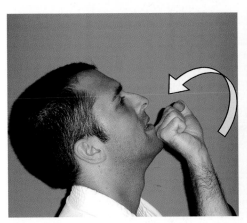
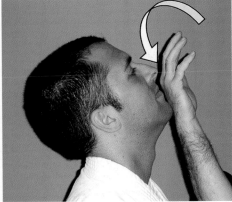

In this case it is better to hit with the open hand, which is loose and closes on contact. These techniques can lead to dazedness and loss of consciousness. They also cause a good deal of pain and can result in serious injury. Once again, extreme care should be taken when practicing the Bunkai.

1.10 Throws (Nage Waza), Foot Sweeps (Ashi Waza), Reaps (Gari Waza)

Manji Gamae from Jion, Bassai Dai, Kanku Dai, Sochin

The Manji Gamae movement out of the abovementioned Kata is not only to be interpreted as a lock but also as the opening to a throw.

Sequence out of the Manji Gamae Kata

Opening to shoulder throw

Lever

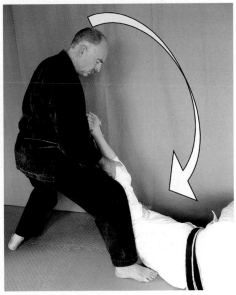

Throw and submission

Unsu, Wankan

Some Kata contain the Nekoashi (Cat Stance). In many cases this stance can be used to initiate a foot sweep or reap. Pressure to the back of the calf at the level of Bladder 57 or 56 (Bl 57, 56) facilitates the technique.

Sequence out of the Kata Unsu

Ude Garami (Upper arm lock)

Opening to a reap, as with O Soto Gari

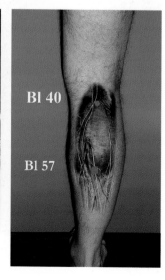

Bl 40

Bl 57

Detailed view for the correct point of pressure

Hold down and control by using lock

Meikyu

Another lock can be found in the Meikyu Kata, which in the Omote (obvious explanation) is generally interpreted as a powerful block with a throw. The following gives an additional hidden explanation (Okuden).

Sequence out of the Kata:Tai Otoshi *Lock on the attacking arm*

Turning in Zenkutsu Dachi, throw with Tai Otoshi, Submission on the floor and continue

With this technique it is essential to direct the eyes far to the left to improve balance. Looking at the falling opponent (as shown) can cause stumbling or losing your footing.

Bassai Dai

The Bassai Dai Kata also contains a hidden foot sweep, as shown in the following. Instead of starting by drawing up the knee for a blow (Hiza Geri), the beginning can also be an Ashi Barai.

Sequence out of the Kata: Starting movement

E.g.: Cross-gripping of the wrist Application: Kake, pulling the arm to the right hip and Ashi Barai (foot sweep)

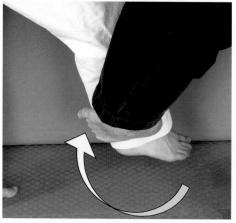

Detailed view of foot sweep Ashi Barai

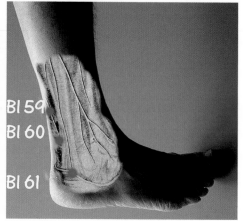

BI 59
BI 60
BI 61

This sweep can also be used to activate the following acupuncture points: Bladder 57 and 58 (BL 59 to 61).

Kanku Sho, Bassai Sho

Another variation of Tai Otoshi is to be found in the abovementioned Kata.

Sequence out of the Kata: This should be Okinawan Kokutsu

Application: Tai Otoshi or Foot Reap

1.11 Lock and Choke (Shime Waza)

Tekki (Naihanchi)

The three Tekki Kata contain numerous techniques for close-quarter fighting. On the surface (Omote), Kage Tsuki is a blow with the fist. A less well-known variation (Okuden) can be interpreted as a choking technique.

Sequence out of the Kata: Kage Tsuki   *Used as a choking technique*

The Kage Tsuki technique also has several other applications and meanings, some of which are described elsewhere in this book.

Jion, Jiin, Jitte

These Kata show the starting phase as a choking technique.

Kata opening scene: Yoi, Jiai No Kamae

Choking technique from behind, counter pressure by placing the head in the opponent's neck

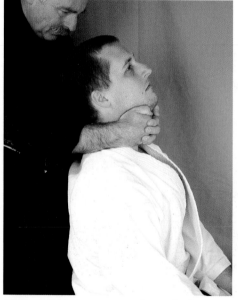

Sitting, counter pressure from the knee

Heian Godan, Kanku Dai

The Juji Uke technique can also be interpreted and applied as a choking technique in these two Kata.

Cross-block with open hands

Gripping and pulling

Nami Juji Jime, gripping both lapels

Drawing in, pressure to the Carotid with open hands

Drawing-in increases pressure to the artery

2 Principles in the Kata

In the interest of increasing Karate's effectiveness, several fundamental principles were adopted from ancient Chinese teachings on health and training. Knowledge of the energy flow in one's own body, which flows through numerous channels in the same way as blood moves through our veins, has had substantial influence on the training methods of the Martial Arts. This knowledge, in particular, was incorporated into the Kata and physical exercises.

Roughly one thousand years ago experts began to concern themselves with energy phenomena capable of influencing the human body. These experts were known in China as Lohan, or "holy men," and they were said to possess superhuman qualities. Statues erected in their honor show positions credited with being able to significantly influence the flow of energy, according to various Qigong institutes in China. An understanding of how to influence the Qi has relevance to areas of daily life, such as Chinese Medicine, exercise for health and well-being and, of course, training methods for the Martial Arts. Qigong, too, was built on the basis of this knowledge.

It is no coincidence that Qigong also contains a Shaolin style, a Daoist style and the Crane style. Qigong has taught us that incorrect training can be the cause of physical discomfort and disorders, surfacing as feelings of increased pressure in the head, pain or insomnia. In China this "energy disorder" is known as Pien Za. Energy lost to others is called Lou Qi. Training which is too concentrated can lead to another malfunction known as the "great confusion" or the "great disorder", which the Chinese call Ching Gong. In addition, we know that training which is too extreme can damage muscles, ligaments and joints and potentially the entire body. In the White Crane Style, hard Qigong training is limited to concentrating on certain main points during the initial years of practice. It is later replaced by soft Qigong training. Similar rules should be maintained and practiced in Karate and Kata training to avoid the abovementioned risk of health disorders, injury and bodily harm.

2.1   Ju and Go (Tai no Shinshuku)

It is crucial in Karate to alternate the use of soft and hard techniques, a principle which arises from understanding the opposing energies of Yin and Yang. It is not especially effective to try to counter a hard attack with a hard block as the use of hard techniques only results in damage to the body. It is, therefore, more constructive to combine and use various elements, such as a soft defense to deflect the attack, in this example. The Goju Ryu (which goes back to the old Naha Te) particularly embraces these rules and contains many forms which utilize the contrasts of hard and soft. We also find numerous Kata in Shotokan Karate which have opposing elements such as in Niju Shi Ho, for example. Once again, one should keep these training principles in mind in order to avoid physical injury when practicing the Kata.

2.2   Rhythm (Waza no Kankyu)

Another principle of importance in the Kata is the rhythm of the movement segments. Whether in combat or training, merely reeling off movements is not going to lead to success. There is no soul in the Kata. The movements themselves are predictable and seemingly innocuous. However, every Kata has its own rhythm which can be interpreted according to its constitution. An opponent can only be caught by surprise if the rhythm of movement is constantly changing. Slow movements have to be followed by fast, hard attacks.

2.3   Using the Flow of Energy

As described at the start, our energy comes through our feet from contact with the earth. We push ourselves away from the ground like a sprinter and build up speed. If our body mass becomes or remains fixed, we can only gather our energy by increasing speed $e = mv^2$. The energy we have drawn from heaven and earth needs to leave the body directed at the opponent. One's own physical center of gravity (Tandien) is the decisive point of transfer. Certain Goju Ryu Kata, such as Sanchin and Tensho, return the energy back into the body through the closed fists for training purposes. This energy feedback to one's inner body is aided by a special breathing technique to achieve a quicker build up of physical power and concentration in Hara (harmony point of the body 3-4 inches below the navel). There are, however, concerns that this special form of training can lead to health problems such as high blood pressure, if used too often and too intensively. For this reason these Kata are practiced in other styles with open hands, in line with the original Chinese model. This also underscores the importance of the responsibility one has toward one's students to ensure that they train correctly. This helps prevent potential health problems. We need to adhere to the Old rules that have been handed down for training and which stress the importance of having knowledge of their relationship to ancient Chinese Medicine.

2.4   There is No Block in Karate

Funakoshi's remark was dealt with in a previous Special Section. According to the principles of Jintai Kyusho, every block should hit a sensitive point in the acupuncture system. This implies that every defense, in effect, should cause the opponent to react in such a way that it facilitates a follow-up attack. A defensive hit to PC 6 (Pericard 6) on the inner side of the forearm, will have such an effect on other points of attack that the heart-circulatory system can be paralyzed. PC 6 can, for example, be struck in Soto Ude Uke. Grips to this type of point are also possible when the fingers are used like pincer tips, as in Chin Na. Blocks to points on the leg can cause the leg to become numb and effectively weaken the opponent for a period of time. Adhering to these principles in a block increases the effectiveness of a technique without undue exertion. This was, and still is, the secret of the old Okinawan Masters who were usually able to retain their fighting strength well into a very advanced age. Decreasing strength, speed and ability to react, in later years, can be well compensated for through knowledge of these technical secrets.

2.5 Touching One's Own Body during the Kata

Karate training is always carried out in bare feet. This is done to intentionally massage the points on the soles of the feet corresponding with various organs (as described earlier in the book). Similar points are, of course, on the surface of the hands and the entire body. There is constant contact with one's own body during the Kata. When correctly executed, this results in stimulation of the meridians which carry the flow of energy throughout the body. This massage principle applies not only to the unarmed Kata but also to forms practiced with various weapons made of wood. Hirokazu Kanazawa described the Ju Ho no Kata, a Kata with the wooden Nunchaku, as a method for promoting one's own health. In this case he is making a reference to a self-massage with the Nunchaku which improves bodily functions and the level of energy. It relieves muscle pain and stiffness of the joints as well. This combination — of achieving physical balance and stimulation of particular acupuncture points — serves to strengthen the muscles and make them more flexible.

2.6 The Circle and the Proper Angle

Sensei Tetsuhiro Hokama's response, when asked about the nature of Karate was: "Karate consists of a circle and 45°." Karate movements are either segments of a circle or in a straight line. Many defensive moves are circular, particularly in the form using softer techniques, as they are ideal for use in countering a hard attack. Circular movements take advantage of the accelerating force of the opponent. That is why many locks and techniques in Aikido start with circular motions. Tuite techniques also have combinations of small and large circles combined with locks at 90° and 30°. There are significant differences between Shuri Te and Naha Te regarding the movements of the feet on the floor. Naha Te (today's Goju Ryu) has typical semi-circular movements. Good defensive movements, independent of strength, can be executed at an angle of 45°. Similar angles are also to be found in Karate's evasive movements (Tai Sabaki). It is surprising to note that almost all sensitive points in Jintai Kyusho are best stimulated at a 45° angle. This probably has to do with the fact that nerve ends on the surface of the body react like piezoelectric elements and anatomically can only be irritated at a certain angle. Examples of this are in the section in which Jintai Kyusho techniques are described. Almost all sensitive points on the head, neck and body react most acutely to an attack at 45°.

2.7 The Meaning Behind a Preparatory Movement

Karate is a very efficient form of combat which has no superfluous movements. However, to a novice, any given preparatory movement may seem to have no particular significance. An advanced student comes to view these moves in a completely different light. Each and every preparatory movement is, in itself, a diverting action for the attacker, the opening to a lock, a throw or a hand grip supporting the next technique. Karate allows no excess movements. Its efficiency enables one to end the fight in the fastest way possible. Attack and defense can only be fast when movement itself is quick, straight-to-the-point and effective. This is important for the beginner to understand and appreciate.

Literature

Abernethy, I. (2006). *Bunkai-Jutsu: The practical application of karate kata.* Neth Publishing in Association with Summersdale Publishers Ltd.

Cardwell, R. (2003). *The western Bubishi. An advanced study of martial science.* Vol 1. Noxville Tennessee: Ludlow Distribution Company.

Clark, R. (2001). *Pressure point fighting. A guide to the secret heart of Asian martial arts.* Boston: Tuttle Publishing.

Croft, A. (2003). *Secret karate, the hidden pressure point techniques of kata.* Ramsburry: Crowood Press Ltd.

Dillman, G. & Thomas C. (1992). *Kyusho jitsu. The Dillman method of pressure point fighting.* Reading USA: Dillman Karate Int. Book.

Dillman, G. & Thomas C. (1994). *Advanced pressure point fighting of Ryukyyu Kempo.* Reading USA: Dillman Karate Int. Book.

Dillman, G. & Thomas C. (1995). *Advanced pressure point grappling.* Tuite Reading USA: Dillman Karate Int. Book.

Fromm, M. (2003). *Vitalpunktstimulation in den Kampfkünsten.* Edition Budo Studien Kreis. Norderstedt: Books on Demand.

Funakoshi, G. (1922, reprint 1997). *To-Te Jitsu.* Hamilton: Masters Publication.

Funakoshi, G. (1981). *Karate-Dô: My way of life.* Tokyo: Kodansha International Ltd.

Funakoshi, G. (1984). *Karate-Dô Kyohan. The master text.* Tokyo: Kodansha International Ltd.

Funakoshi, G. (1988, reprint 1994). *Karate-Dô nyumon.* Tokyo: Kodansha International Ltd.

Funakoshi, G. (2001). *Karate jutsu: The original teachings of Master Funakoshi.* Tokyo: Kodansha International Ltd.

Funakoshi, G. (2003). *The twenty guiding principles of karate.* Tokyo: Kodansha International Ltd.

Habersetzer, R. (2004). *Bubishi. An der Quelle des Karatedô.* Chemnitz: Palisander Verlag.

Habersetzer, R. (2005). *Koshiki Kata, die klassische Kata des Karate Do.* Chemnitz: Palisander Verlag.

Higaonna, M. (1995). *Traditional karatedo, Okinawa Goju-Ryu,* Vol. 4. Applications of the Kata Part 2. Tokyo: Sugawara Martial Arts Institute, Inc.

Hokama, T. (1984). *Okinawa Karate no Ayumi* (History of Okinawa karate). Okinawa, Japan.

Hokama, T. (1997). *History and traditions of Okinawan karate.* Hamilton, Ontario, Canada: Masters Publication.

Hokama, T. (2006). *100 masters of Okinawa karate.* Okinawa Japan: Ozato Print Co. Okinawa.

Hokama, T. (2007). *Timeline of karate history.* Okinawa Japan: Ozato Print Co. Okinawa.

Hokama, T. (2008). *Classical Okinawan Goju-Ryu Karate-Jutsu.* (Vol 1). Knoxville Tenessee: Bushido Press.

Jwing-Ming, Y. (1995). *Comprehensive applications of Shaolin Chin Na, the practical defence of Chinese seizing arts for all styles.* Roslindale: YMAA Publication Center.

Jwing-Ming, Y. (1996). *The essence of Shaolin White Crane, martial power and qigong.* Roslindale: YMAA Publication Center.

Jwing-Ming, Y. (2004). *Analysis of Shaolin Chin Na, instructor's manual for all martial styles.* Roslindale: YMAA Publicaation Center.

Kane, L. & Wilder, K. (2005). *The way of kata. A comprehensive guide to deciphering martial applications.* Boston: YMAA Publication Center Inc.

Keller, G. (2006). *Bubishi, Handbuch der Karate-Kampfkunst.* Frankfurt: Angkor Verlag.

Kelly, M. (2001). *Death touch: The science behind the legend of Dim Mac.* Boulder, Colorado: Paladin Press.

Kerr, G. H. (2000). *Okinawa: The history of an island people.* Tokyo: Tuttle Publishing.

Kirby, G. (2001). *Jujitsu nerve techniques, the invisible weapon of self-defence.* Lubock, TX: Ohara Publications Inc.

König, G. & Wancura I. (1975). *Neue Chinesische Akupunktur. Lehrbuch und Atlas mit naturwissenschaftlichen Erklärungen.* Wien: Verlag Wilhelm Maudrich.

Lind, W. (1977). *Okinawa Karate.* Berlin: Sportverlag Berlin GmbH.

Martinez, J. (2001). *Okinawan karate, the secret art of Tuite.* San Juan, Porto Rico: First Book Publishing of P. R.

McCarthy, P. (1987). *Classic kata of Okinawan karate.* Santa Clarita, California: Ohara Publ. Inc.

McCarthy, P. (1995). *The bible of karate. Bubishi.* Boston: Tuttle Publishing.

McCarthy, P. (1999). *Ancient Okinawan martial arts, Koryu Uchinadi.* Boston: Tuttle Publishing.

Measara, J. (2002). *Karate Kata no Rekishi, die Geschichte der Karate Katas.* Kelly-Druck GmbH, 93326 Abensberg.

Montaigue, E. (1993). *Dim Mak: Death point striking.* Boulder, Colorado: Paladin Press.

Montaigue, E. (1995). *Dim Mak's 12 most deadly katas. Points of no Return.* Boulder, Colorado: Paladin Press.

Montaigue, E. & Simpson, W. (1997). *The encyclopedia of Dim Mac: The extra meridians, points, and more.* Boulder, Colorado: Paladin Press.

Montaigue, E. & Simpson, W. (1997). *The encyclopedia of Dim Mac: The main meridians.* Boulder, Colorado: Paladin Press.

Motobu, C. (1926, reprint 1995). *Okinawan Karate Kempo.* Masters Publication. Hamilton, Ontario, Canada.

Nagamine, S. (1976). *Okinawan Karate Do.* C. E. Tokyo: Tuttle Publ. Inc.

Rohen, J. W. (2001). *Funktionelle Neuroanatomie.* Stuttgart: Schattauer Verlag.

Reinisch, St., Höller J. & Maluschka A. (2009). *Kyusho, Angriffspunkte in Selbstverteidigung und Kampfsport.* Aachen: Meyer & Meyer Verlag.

Sakon, M. K. (2005). *The secret royal martial arts of Ryukyu.* GmbH Norderstedt, Germany: Books on Demand.

Stux, G., Stiller N., Berman B. & Pomeranz B. (2003). *Akupunktur, Lehrbuch und Atlas.* Berlin: Springer-Verlag.

Tedeschi, M. (2003). *Essential anatomy for healing & martial arts.* Weatherhill, New York, Tokyo.

Walker, A. F. & Bauer C. (2002). *The ancient art of life and death: The book of Dim Mak.* Boulder, Colorado: Paladin Press.

Whichello Brown, D. (2004). *Fuß Reflexzonen Massage. Alle Techniken Schritt für Schritt.* Köln: Bellavista.

Whichello Brown, D. (2004). *Hand Reflexzonen Massage. Schmerzen lindern – Vitalität steigern.* Köln: Bellavista.

Zhong, Jun Jing (1934, reprint 2006). *Dian Xue Shu. Skill of acting on acupoints.* USA: Lulu Press.

Internet

www.budokaj.de
www.budoelite.com

Credits

Photography:	Helmut Kogel
Cover Photos:	Helmut Kogel; © artcalin/Fotolia.com
Cover Design:	Sabine Groten
Editing:	Martha Tuninga

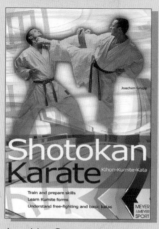